KU-612-503

Getting into

Veterinary School

Emily Lucas
12th edition

Francis Holland School NW1 6XR

T4251

Getting into guides

Getting into Art & Design Courses, 11th edition
Getting into Business & Economics Courses, 14th edition
Getting into Dental School, 11th edition
Getting into Engineering Courses, 6th edition
Getting into Law, 13th edition
Getting into Medical School: 2022 Entry, 26th edition
Getting into Oxford & Cambridge: 2022 Entry, 24th edition
Getting into Pharmacy and Pharmacology Courses, 2nd edition
Getting into Physiotherapy Courses, 10th edition
Getting into Psychology Courses, 13th edition
Getting into Veterinary School, 12th edition
How to Complete Your UCAS Application: 2022 Entry, 33rd edition

Getting into Veterinary School

This 12th edition published in 2021 by Trotman Education, an imprint of Trotman Publishing Ltd, 21d Charles Street, Bath BA1 1HX

© Trotman Publishing Ltd 2021

Author: Emily Lucas
7th–11th edns: James Barton
5th–6th edns: Mario De Clemente
3rd–4th edns: James Burnett
1st–2nd edns: John Handley (published in 1999 as *Getting into Veterinary Science*)

Editions 1–6 published by Trotman and Co. Ltd

British Library Cataloguing in Publication Data
A catalogue record for this book is available from the British Library.

ISBN 978 1 912943 40 1

All rights reserved. This book is sold subject to the condition that it shall not, by way of trade or otherwise, be lent, resold, hired out or otherwise circulated without the publisher's prior written consent in any form of binding or cover other than that in which it is published and without a similar condition including this condition being imposed on the subsequent purchaser. No part of this publication may be reproduced, stored in a retrieval system or transmitted in any form or by any means, electronic and mechanical, photocopying, recording or otherwise without prior permission of Trotman Publishing.

Printed and bound in the UK by Ashford Colour Press Ltd

Contents

About the author

Emily Lucas read medical science at the University of Birmingham before obtaining a master's degree in genomic medicine at Queen Mary, University of London. She currently holds the position of University Support Officer and helps students with their university applications, as well as supporting students with pre-admissions tests, such as the University Clinical Aptitude Test (UCAT) and the BioMedical Admissions Test (BMAT). As well as teaching, Emily has maintained a research position at the University of Birmingham in the field of epigenetics. Emily also teaches biology, and is the current author of Trotman's *Getting into Law* guide, and co-author of the *Getting into Dental School* and *Getting into Medical School* guides.

Acknowledgements

I would like to thank everybody who has contributed to the twelfth edition of *Getting into Veterinary School*, including MPW and Trotman Education for giving me the opportunity to write it.

I would like to thank all of the individuals who have contributed to the book, especially Grace Holmes, Marie Kubiak, Jade Ramsay, Melisa Kalkan, Mary Cecelia, Briony Milner, James Hollis and Georgia Owen for their insights into applying to, studying and working in the field of veterinary medicine. In addition, I would like to thank James Hollis, Georgia Owen, Maria Lyons and former contributors for allowing me to reproduce their personal statements here as successful examples. I am extremely grateful that these individuals were willing to take time out of their busy schedules to contribute.

I would also like to thank those at UCAS and the Royal College of Veterinary Surgeons, as well as the university admissions departments, who have supported me by answering questions and providing statistics.

Emily Lucas

Introduction
'Do I have a cat in hell's chance?!'

If you're running around like a headless chicken or feel like a fish out of water when it comes to your veterinary school application, then this book will help you get to grips with each aspect of it, and give you an insight into the realities of being a veterinarian. There is truth in the idiom that the early bird catches the worm. A successful application to veterinary school requires meticulous planning, reflection on your work experience and a thorough understanding of what the profession entails, so by starting your application early, you will give yourself the best chance of gaining a place. Relate to the tortoise and not the hare, as last-minute applications are rarely successful. And remember, stay positive – every dog does have its day!

All right, enough animal clichés for now, but it is important that you note that while the process of applying to veterinary schools will help to shape your future career choice, you should never let it get to the stage where it grinds you down. Aside from anything else, by the end of this book, you should have an answer to the feline question above and be the one who got the cream instead of using up one of your nine lives! And so to business.

About this book

Someone once said to me: 'If you are allergic to animals, being a vet might not be the best career path.' This might sound like a ridiculous statement, but it does make a half-decent point: make sure your career decision is well thought out. Applications to veterinary school are competitive, with a success rate of around 18% in the UK. In 2020, there were 9,765 applications (compared to 10,140 in 2019) for pre-clinical veterinary medicine at veterinary school; of these, 1,765 (compared to 1,415 in the previous cycle) were accepted.

For those aspiring to join the veterinary profession, the most important question is 'What can I do to make sure that I am in that 18% when I apply?' The aim of this book is to supply you with that information. However, there is no secret formula that will ensure success. The students who are accepted work hard to gain their places. They are motivated and determined, and their desire to work in the field of veterinary science is deep-rooted and genuine. Having said that, without adequate preparation, even the most promising candidate will not get a place if they do not fulfil the required criteria.

This book serves as a guide to help you with the complexities of a veterinary application. Like veterinary surgery, ample preparation is required, alongside an attention to detail, good knowledge, and with all the variables working together.

How to use this book

The competition for places on a veterinary science degree course is ferocious, and the odds of getting in are not as favourable as on other courses. For example, for 2018/19 entry, the Royal Veterinary College (RVC) made 395 offers to 2,520 applicants. As you will see from Tables 1 and 7 (pages 3 and 174), applicant numbers are high, so you are going to need to prepare thoroughly for this application, taking into consideration all aspects of the course in order to maximise your opportunity of studying veterinary medicine at university.

This book will discuss all aspects of the application, from how to research and prepare for your application, choosing your course and the application itself, to the interview, results day and information on fees and funding. In Chapter 8 there is advice and information for 'non-standard' applicants – mature students, graduates and retake students. We also look at potential careers within veterinary medicine, and, at the end of the book, there is a further information section and a glossary where you will find details of sources for veterinary medicine and definitions of any abbreviations relevant to your UCAS application for veterinary courses.

The twelve chapters discuss the following:

1. The bare necessities: What is the role of a vet?
2. Horses for courses: Studying veterinary medicine
3. Separating the sheep from the goats: Preparation and experience
4. The 'Jack Russell' Group: Choosing your course
5. Take the bull by the horns in the cattle market: The UCAS application
6. No one likes a copycat: The personal statement
7. So why did the chicken cross the road? The interview
8. A leopard does not change its spots: Non-standard applicants
9. A bird in the hand: Results day
10. Counting sheep: Financing your course
11. Snakes and ladders: Careers paths
12. Don't count your chickens before they've hatched: Further information.

Table 1 UCAS End of Cycle applicant statistics for Pre-clinical Veterinary Medicine 2010–2020

Year	Total			UK			EU			Non-EU		
	Applications	Acceptances	Ratio of Applications: Acceptances	Applications	Acceptances	Ratio of Applications: Acceptances	Applications	Acceptances	Ratio of Applications: Acceptances	Applications	Acceptances	Ratio of Applications: Acceptances
2020	9,765	1,765	5.5	7,515	1,400	5.4	1,065	85	12.5	1,190	280	4.3
2019	10,140	1,415	7.2	8,045	1,145	7.0	1,045	45	23.2	1,055	225	4.7
2018	9,165	1,280	7.2	7,240	1,005	7.2	965	40	24.1	950	235	4.0
2017	7,435	1,175	6.3	5,775	965	6.0	855	30	28.5	805	180	4.5
2016	7,935	1,215	6.5	6,075	995	6.1	1,050	35	30.0	810	185	4.4
2015	8,335	1,165	7.2	6,360	990	6.4	1,160	25	46.4	815	150	5.4
2014	8,965	1,075	8.3	7,170	905	7.9	1,055	15	70.3	740	155	4.8
2013	9,040	1,010	9.0	7,210	825	8.7	1,010	15	67.3	820	170	4.8
2012	8,780	1,020	8.6	7,010	845	8.3	970	15	64.7	800	160	5.0
2011	8,190	970	8.4	6,655	765	8.7	1,010	15	67.3	525	190	2.8
2010	8,150	980	8.3	6,545	780	8.4	1,090	20	54.5	515	180	2.9

Source: www.ucas.com
We acknowledge UCAS' contribution of this information.

Chapter 1 looks at the fundamentals of being a vet: what is involved, what skills and qualities you need to have and the nature of the work.

Chapter 2 discusses the different types of veterinary medicine course available, focusing on each stage of the degree and looking in depth at the different universities offering this course, analysing what their unique features are for each stage.

Chapter 3 explores the practical aspect of the preparation for an application, i.e. work experience and what each university requires. It looks at the different types of work experience and why such a variety of work experience is required.

Chapter 4 examines further the factors you might wish to consider when choosing a course and the grade requirements for each university.

Chapter 5 walks you through the application itself: admissions tests, deadlines, transferring from one course to another and what to do next.

Chapter 6 is an in-depth look at the personal statement and how it should be written, including what to include and things to avoid submitting.

Chapter 7 discusses the interview stage, possible questions to expect and includes a detailed commentary on topical animal illnesses as noted by the government in 2020.

Chapter 8 addresses international applications, overseas universities, mature students and special educational needs provision in the application process.

Chapter 9 looks at what happens on results day itself and what you will need to do if resits are required. It looks at re-applications and gives guidance on what steps you should take next.

Chapter 10 delves into the financial aspects of the course, looking at the cost of veterinary school, including what equipment is required, and then discusses loans and other financing options.

Chapter 11 gives more details about the range of careers you can pursue in veterinary medicine and what you can specialise in after your degree course; accreditation; the importance of people skills and a professional attitude. It then offers a general summation of the application.

Chapter 12 summarises the acronyms used and refers you to other sources of information that you might wish to look at while making an application.

As with other books in this series, this book is designed as a guide to the application process as opposed to a guide to the profession. Your work experience is your opportunity to find out more about being a vet.

This book should in no way be seen as dissuasive. It is about getting into veterinary school – it is not designed to put you off and push you towards something else. The tone reflects a balanced mixture of realism and optimism. No one should underestimate the hard road that lies ahead. Getting into one of the ten veterinary schools in the UK (including the newly established schools, Aberystwyth and Harper & Keele) is just the first stage on the route to becoming a qualified veterinary surgeon, with all the inevitable hard work and dedication that will follow in the next 40 years or so. The key to success lies within each individual.

Academic ability is not merely a requirement; it is an absolute necessity. Unless you have the clear potential to study science in the sixth form, this book alone cannot help you. Students attracted to veterinary science should have a natural academic ability in the sciences. A confident prediction of high grades at A level is a great help, but even that will not be enough on its own to get into one of the veterinary schools. You will have to show proof of your interest, enthusiasm and commitment – you will have to show that this is what you really want.

So how do you know that this is the career for you? If you are asking yourself this, your number one priority must be to become well enough informed about and acquainted with the work of a vet to ensure that you have made the right choice of career and to safeguard against regrets further down the line. And once you know this, what do you need to consider next?

- What are the factors involved in choosing a course? Have you considered all of them?
- What do the courses have in common?
- What are the factors that influence admissions tutors to come down in favour of one well-qualified candidate over another?
- What happens at interview?
- What about the various career choices open to the newly qualified vet?
- What do customers who use the services of a veterinary surgeon look for in a 'good' vet?
- Does this sound like the kind of profession that would suit you?

Putting academic skill to one side for a moment, would you feel comfortable dealing with your customers as well as with the animals? The first thing you learn in veterinary practice is that all animals bring an owner with them. How would you handle a sceptical Dalesman or an elderly lady who is anxious and watchful as you come into contact with her beloved pet? Animals play a crucial part in the lives of their owners and whether the vet handles this with tact and understanding will be the deciding factor in both their professional and their personal development. This book will help those who feel drawn to the career for sentimental reasons to understand the realities – good and bad – of being a vet and will enable you to evaluate whether you have what it takes to follow this path.

A feature of this book is real students' views. Many people who are now undergraduates on veterinary courses say that they would have appreciated knowing the views of people in their position when they were at school. Panels of students returning to their former schools to give careers advice often do not include a veterinary student. This book, therefore, includes several student profiles, the first of which is given below.

Case study

Melissa is studying at the Royal Veterinary College (RVC).

'I always wanted to be a veterinarian. In Turkey we have a lot of stray animals and my family and I used to take care of them ever since I was a little kid. This made me grow up with so much love towards animals. This love that I have for animals really kept me going throughout my whole journey to finally get into a vet uni.

'In my personal statement I talked about all the work experience I had done and not only how it helped me understand the whole veterinary world better but also made me grow as a person. I also talked about how I faced some challenges along the way and saw the not so nice sides of becoming a vet (such as, during work experience in Africa, having to put healthy dogs down simply because their owners didn't have enough money to take care of them), and how these challenges have encouraged me – rather than bringing my motivation down – to do more research professionally once I graduate to find better alternatives for the animals.

'The way I prepared for my interview was that I read so much about the common topics (this I feel is a very important thing as in all my interviews they asked me so much about these topics and my experience of/views on them). I had answers prepared for why I wanted to become a veterinarian, as well as why that uni was one of my choices. This sounds quite simple. However, to be able to stand out from others, I actually spent a lot of time preparing my answers.

'I talked about how becoming a vet opens up so many doors, and that I was well aware that it's not only about opening a clinic. I felt they quite liked it when I told them vets could even work for normal human doctors due to zoonotic diseases; work with soldiers for war animals; work in research labs, agriculture, slaughter houses; with psychologists; and everything you can think of, as animals affect many things we don't often think about.

'I also did quite a lot of research as to why that uni was different from all the other ones. This can be in terms of how it structures its course, the facilities it has on campus, different opportunities it can help you with, and so on.

'In all of my interviews I made a few small mistakes that I wish I could go back to and correct. However, I tried not to think about them and move on as soon as possible as I couldn't change what was already done/said and this was only going to affect my other answers in a negative way. I feel like this really helped me.

'During the interviews, I found that even if they ask you an obvious question, they often want you to give more than just the answer to their question. In other words, those questions are there to lead you in a certain way and make you talk about that topic.

'A good example to this was during my Bristol interview. They gave me a scenario where I found an injured badger and they asked me what I would do. To begin with I answered their question by simply saying I would take it to the vet as I wasn't qualified to help them. But then I continued and told them I would also look at what kind of injury it was, and if it looked like a gunshot then I would contact the RSPCA, as during my interview time a new law was introduced for badger culling and people were allowed to shoot them but only if they were locked in a cage, to make sure that they were actually dead instead of suffering. The interviewer said this was a very good answer as I had expanded on more than what they just asked for.

'I applied to Surrey, Nottingham, RVC and Bristol and got an interview from all of them except Surrey. I ended up choosing RVC as my firm choice as I really like the referral hospital there and I thought that was the correct place for me to learn as my goal is to open my own animal hospital after I graduate. Nottingham was my insurance choice because they teach with a lot of practicals and I feel like I learn best that way.

'I got an offer from all of my interviews.

'I did my A levels in one year instead of two as I moved to England the year before the syllabus change. It was a really tough year for me as I was doing three science subjects in a very limited time. I can't count the amount of times I thought I wouldn't make it, but dreaming of my future as a vet kept me motivated.

'I found the easiest way to study was by doing past papers, as after a while I started to understand what each question type was aiming to get out of students. There were some long answer questions that I even learned the mark schemes for as it was just like an exemplar essay answer.

'I was offered AAA but I got AA in my biology and psychology and a B in my chemistry and still managed to get into RVC. This made me fully realise the importance of interviews and personal statements.

'Once I started at RVC, I found that the first week was the hardest as there is a big change in teaching method from A levels to university. I felt like I was constantly confused during my lectures as I was trying to write down everything and this wasn't possible as the lecturers talk very quickly. After a while I started doing prep before my lectures and this was really helpful for me and I gained my confidence back.

'Our lecturers in RVC upload the PowerPoints online before the lecture. What I do is I write down all the learning objectives of the lecture and write down only the relevant parts of the PowerPoint under each of these learning objectives and during the lecture if the lecturer explains something else that is not written in the PowerPoint then I note it down under the relevant learning objective.

'The lecturers keep telling us that we can't possibly learn everything and every single learning objective for any of our exams, unlike A levels. Instead, what we have to do is learn some of them and do further reading about those ones.'

Fact: Almost half the pigs in the world are kept by farmers in China.

1 | The bare necessities
What is the role of a vet?

This is perhaps the most pertinent question of all because the answer to that question reflects the considerable sacrifice in terms of time and effort that every vet makes. Every veterinary practice has to be organised so that someone is on call 24 hours a day, for 365 days a year. As one farmer commented: 'A vet needs to have a really good sense of humour to be called out at 3 a.m. on a cold night to deal with a difficult calving and having to get down in six inches of muck!' It is certainly not a career for someone lacking in confidence, or who holds back and carries an air of uncertainty. Vets are still held in high esteem. The popular image of a vet is of someone working long hours, who is able and caring, whose charges are not too high, and who doesn't worry too much about bills being paid promptly! While this closing sentiment might be ambitious, the popular view is in fact the accurate view.

James Herriot, an English veterinary surgeon and writer, would probably do these words more justice at this stage: he reveals in his books what the profession really entails. In his first book, *If Only They Could Talk*, he reflects on the unpredictability of animals and indeed a vet's life as a whole: 'It's a long tale of little triumphs and disasters,' writes Herriot, 'and you've got to really like it to stick it ... One thing, you never get bored.'

On another occasion, Herriot muses, with aching ribs and bruises all over his legs, that being a vet is, in fact, a strange way to earn a living.

> 'But then I might have been in an office with the windows tight shut against the petrol fumes and the traffic noise, the desk light shining on the columns of figures, my bowler hat hanging on the wall. Lazily I opened my eyes again and watched a cloud shadow riding over the face of the green hill across the valley. No, no . . . I wasn't complaining.'

Some people grumble about the beguiling influence of the Herriot books. There is, however, a lot of cool reality in the pages laden with good humour and philosophy; so much so that one student described the effect of the books as leaving a 'cold afterglow'. Many professions would love to have a PR agent with the skills of Herriot writing on their behalf.

The role of the vet is far more than just scientific curiosity. For large parts, the role of the vet is about education; not only of the self through ongoing continuous professional development (CPD) but, more specifically, of the owners and the public. Prevention over cure in some cases. A lot of animal-based diseases spread very quickly because herds, for example, are often densely packed. As such, it is vital that a vet advises on appropriate animal husbandry, not just with large animals, but within the home as well. An equally important part of the role is to help new pet owners understand the needs of small animals and how to look after them – not dissimilar from understanding how to look after a child for the first time.

CPD is incredibly important throughout your career. The Royal College of Veterinary Surgeons' (RCVS) Code of Professional Conduct for Veterinary Surgeons maintains that, as a practising veterinary surgeon, you have a responsibility to 'maintain and develop the knowledge and skills relevant to your professional practice and competence'; i.e. make sure you are up to date for the welfare of the animals ultimately. A minimum amount of 35 hours of CPD per year is required for veterinary surgeons, though this should always be regarded as the bottom of the scale and the more you do, the more confident you will be that you are fully aware of all developments in the profession. The RCVS recently updated their CPD platform, which encourages reflective practice, with this element becoming compulsory from January 2022. Amid the Coronavirus pandemic, the annual CPD requirement was reduced by 25% to 26 hours for 2020, which may be maintained moving forward depending on the lingering impacts of the virus.

The choice is fairly flexible, as long as you can justify its purpose. Some examples are:

- discussion group – informal learning set
- practical training – clinical skills lab
- preparing a new lecture/presentation
- research – veterinary business
- secondment to another workplace
- 'seeing practice' – work-based observation
- training – in house.

'The best thing about this profession is that it affords so much variety; from domestic to exotic animals, from large animals to birds. You are always learning in this job, and the best way to learn is often to teach – a crucial part of a vet's toolbox.'

Dominic (practising vet in the Wirral)

The principal focus of this chapter is on the role of the vet and what is required in order to make you successful.

So what makes a good vet?

- Confidence
- Authority
- Composure
- Nerve
- Empathy – for both patient and client
- Versatility
- Focus
- Organisation
- Resilience
- Being well informed
- Knowing one's limitations
- Good decision-making ability
- Exceptional knowledge
- Good judgement, e.g. prevention versus cure
- And, above all, a thick skin.

If you have these qualities, a career in veterinary medicine is a strong possibility. Vets are incredibly resilient people who deal with a variety of challenges on a weekly, often daily, basis. You must have confidence in your own abilities and your own judgement, but you must also have the strength to communicate effectively and authoritatively. Bear in mind that you will be calling the shots because you will be the expert.

A good vet can diagnose most things, but, if they cannot, it is their job to know who can. The secret is to know your own limitations. This is particularly important for the newly qualified veterinary surgeon. 'New vets,' according to experienced Cheshire farmer David Faulkner, 'must know when to seek help and be mature enough not to be too embarrassed, for there are always a lot of new things still to learn.'

The farmer's view

'Farmers know immediately if they are going to get on with you,' an experienced vet revealed. 'They look at the way you handle and approach the animals. If you can't catch them, the owner will lose confidence and you won't be allowed anywhere near the livestock.' A seasoned farmer confided: 'Give me a vet who doesn't wait to be asked and is out giving you a hand.' He added: 'If they are confident in what they are doing it soon comes across.' Farmers and animal owners generally like to have a vet who communicates well, has a sense of humour, is outgoing rather than shy and reserved, and is able to walk into any situation and have an answer. There is a baseless stigma about women in the profession and the capability of female vets in large-animal situations. The truth of the matter is that if you choose to specialise in this field, gender issues will disappear if you are confident and firm.

Prevention

Even with the technological advances of the 21st century, prevention makes sense. Animals simply cannot tell you when they are unwell, so a good vet will seek to promote preventive medicine whenever possible. Today, there is a lot of knowledge about preventive health by diet and vaccination. Whole herds can be treated at the right time of year. Farmers expect their vet to look ahead and draw their attention to what will prevent disease: 'Look, October is approaching – why not vaccinate all the cattle and prevent pneumonia?' If you give this kind of advice you will inspire faith in those you are seeking to help. Additives can be administered in either feed or drink. This is much better than having to go through the trauma of injecting a whole farmyard of pigs! A vet can do a lot of good with vaccinations and treating deficiencies through the feed by replacing what is not there, improving not only productivity but also the welfare of the animals.

Most people will agree that prevention is better than cure, but sometimes this is a naive statement to make. Preventive medicine is costly, and farmers seeking profits may be more inclined to be frugal. There is no doubt that preventive medicine is a good investment for the future, but in the aftermath of BSE (bovine spongiform encephalopathy), foot-and-mouth disease, and the collapse of much of their export market, farmers are anxious and, in many cases, unwilling to make the necessary outlay. Drug usage for cattle has fallen away. Often farmers do not approach the vet until there is an emergency and by then it might just be an exercise in damage limitation.

In today's busy world, with a general shortage of vets, it is not always easy to respond to this situation. It is said in the profession that you should try to take time to stop and let your eyes range over the flock or herd, looking for the one or two animals that do not fit into the general pattern and who seem out of sorts. There is also a lot to be said for encouraging good husbandry by advising on the housing of the animals. While the sign of a good vet is that they will have the latest drug information at their fingertips and knowledge of how to treat certain conditions, sound, informed and diplomatic advice will often earn the vet similar respect and kudos among their clients: 'Instead of me treating the animals' feet, why don't you improve that footpath?'

Small animals

Working with household animals can require a different approach. It is as much about counselling the owners as treating the patients, and, for that reason, interpersonal skills are a prerequisite. With pets, there is great variety: one moment you might be treating a reptile with a nutritional problem; the next, a cat losing weight might be brought in for tests and cause you to wonder if there might be a problem with its liver – or could it be cancer? A rabbit could be brought in – many are now regarded as house pets – and your initial diagnosis of myxomatosis might be confirmed. Or it could be something as mundane as placing a microchip in an animal for security purposes. Dental problems among the small-animal population occur quite frequently but obesity is also much more common than most people imagine. The vet has to advise and persuade the owner – however obstinate they might be – to reduce the animal's feed and bring it in for regular weigh-ins at the surgery.

A lot of animals are kept in busy urban environments, thus increasing the risk of pets being involved in road accidents. If a dog that has been hit by a vehicle is brought in, the 'crash kit' may have to be used. The doses of the most commonly used drugs are marked clearly on the crash box lid, the syringes are loaded, and everything is sterilised and ready. It is important to act quickly, but the true professional keeps calm; this is no time for the vet to fumble when decisive action can save the dog's life.

Arguably the most important quality required for this job is having a thick skin, especially in cases where an animal has to be euthanised. The ethical issues that affect our medical profession and the moral question of 'playing God' do not exist in the veterinary counterpart because it is often kinder to make these decisions for the good of the animal. You have to weigh up the animal's suffering against the owner's protestations and grief and your own conscience. A good vet must find that little bit extra inside themselves. It is crucial to deal with the owners in a compassionate yet effective way. It has often been said that the hope and trust of the owners are matched only by the trust and helplessness of the animals. Imagine dealing with a distraught child when he's told that his pet hamster must be put down. How do you show empathy amid the boy's flood of tears? How do you discuss it with him? Perhaps the boy's parents will let you attempt to explain how the hamster feels and that soon the small animal's pain will cease and the end itself will not be felt. Even when you know it is the kindest thing to do, giving a lethal injection is still one of the toughest parts of the job.

Large animals

The ability to look after large animals requires a completely different skill set. Firstly, there is the sheer physicality needed to look after these powerful animals. You cannot be timid around large animals as you need to give them confidence so they trust you.

Then there is the farmer. It is important to note that large animals are the livelihood of the owner and, therefore, dealing with farmers requires a certain diplomacy and resolve from you because, as you can appreciate, they are trying to look at the bigger picture and the impact this might have on business. That is not to say they do not also care about their animals, merely that they have a twin focus which often makes it trickier to advise if you feel a cull is required.

There is also the need for you to see these animals in a different way from small animals. Your job is very much to focus on the health and welfare of the animal, to ensure they are well looked after and that they are not in any danger. That said, you must keep in mind that many of these animals are raised for different purposes, i.e. work and food in the case of most herds. You need to understand this and separate any attachment to the animal out from the job.

> 'Forget about the prejudices towards women and size in this profession; that doesn't matter. However, there is a point behind it in terms of the ability to deal with large animals, therefore my advice is to keep yourself fit. Working outside all the time is very healthy but very cold in the winter!'
>
> Rachel (practising vet in Devon)

So why do you want to be a vet?

It's important to ask yourself this because if you become a vet you will be embarking on a career that is extremely challenging. Perhaps for you it is about adapting and fitting into a way of life. Is this what keeps everyone focused during the long hours of study? An interest in and sympathy for animals is taken for granted by many commentators, but in reality it is the way you react to an emergency that puts your dedication to the test. It is all in a day's (or night's) work for a vet and there is no one to applaud you except the grateful, or perhaps less understanding, owner. In short, commitment is the key, particularly if – or perhaps that should be when – the going gets tough. As a vet you must feel that you want to help, cure and take care of animals to the best of your ability, whatever the weather and whatever the circumstances. It is the kind of commitment that will almost certainly have begun at a very early age and will have become stronger and more focused in your teenage and university years. Of course, while the vast majority of qualified vets are in general practice, this is not the only option open to you: you might equally choose to go into teaching, inspection or research. Yet no matter which option you pursue, the level of knowledge and commitment required is very high.

Case study

Briony completed her A levels in Biology, Chemistry and Maths, as well as AS levels in Music and Further Maths, and secured the grades to gain a place on the veterinary medicine course at the University of Liverpool.

'I've always enjoyed working with and being around animals. My mum is a doctor and I knew that I didn't want to follow in her footsteps and pursue a career in medicine, and it was jokingly suggested that I become a vet instead. I seriously considered this option for a while and, after doing a lot of research into what it would involve, really liked the idea. I visited a small-animal practice and, after that, decided that this was definitely the path that I wanted to pursue.

'Before applying, I carried out work experience for many weeks at a variety of surgeries local to me, ranging from small-animal only through to a mixed-equine practice. As I got closer to my application, I used the work experience entry requirements for university courses to guide me on what was needed. I have been lambing on various farms, spent weeks on beef and dairy farms, and worked at stables, kennels and catteries. I also spent a week at the Three Counties Equine Hospital.

'All of the non-clinical experience taught me a lot about handling animals and the differences between species; tramping through fields and being out in all sorts of weather certainly toughens you up, and I definitely know how to dress for cold weather! All work experience really improves your people skills and teaches you how to interact with people from all walks of life and different viewpoints – getting used to communicating with country farmers with thick regional accents is a skill for life. Learning how individuals interact with their animals and how they view them is essential too, as not everyone will have the same opinion as you when it comes to animals. To some people they are just farm animals, while others will be very precious about their herd. Similarly, some owners are obsessive about their pets, while others are more pragmatic. Not enforcing your personal viewpoint and making a client feel judged is an essential skill for a vet, but also a general life skill.

'From a clinical perspective, seeing practice taught me how different teams work and that the environment can vary dramatically in each practice. Seeing the day-to-day job is really important to help you work out whether it is a job that you want to pursue as it is a lot to take on!

'I retook my A levels because of extenuating circumstances beyond my control, which narrowed down my application choices as not all veterinary schools consider applicants in this position.

'Before retaking my exams, I took a gap year where I worked three jobs in order to finance a two-month stay on a sheep ranch in Canada, which ended up becoming three months! If it is an option, I would strongly encourage all veterinary medicine applicants to take a gap year. I learned a lot of life lessons during my two years before starting university and, as a result, felt far more confident in myself. I have never been aware of an age difference, which I know many people worry about when not starting university at 18, and I am far from the oldest person in my year. I have also noticed that a lot of students who join the course straight from A levels tend to find it more difficult. Gaining a bit more maturity and developing your study skills first can be really beneficial.

'Studying veterinary medicine so far has been tough! There are also parts of the course that I haven't really enjoyed so far. There are students who love the entire thing and smile their way through the course, but I am not one of them. The lectures are difficult, the hours are long, and the support can feel minimal. The pressures of stereotypical university life can be hard for many students, especially those who party a bit too hard in first year, but you have to quickly find a balance of work and play! The vet school itself can feel confusing, disorganised and frustrating from a student's point of view. You can get contradicting messages from different lecturers, or even the same lecturer, leaving you lost as to what the best thing to do is. Finding a group of friends on the course can be helpful to discuss these things with – even if you're all as lost as each other, you feel better being lost together! It is a steep learning curve, but you will manage to get through.

'I particularly enjoy the practical aspects of the course. Personally, I find the lectures tough as it isn't how I learn best, although a lot of the content is very interesting. Learning things that are more applicable to the job is always more interesting! The social side of the vet school as a whole has always been enjoyable. We do things for first years in freshers' week which helps everyone to get to know each other and some of the older years too. There are also whole vet school parties and events, which are a great way to let loose.

As well as some of the lectures being really complex, I find the lack of holidays tough, as you have to take on work experience during your breaks rather than term time, which means that you get very few weeks off during the year. Not only is this quite tiring, but it makes it difficult to earn money, which can make university life that bit harder. It also makes having a social life outside of university more difficult as you don't have much time to see your family or friends from home or go on holiday. Of course, this is just part of the course, but it can be frustrating compared to other vocational courses like medicine and dentistry where placements are handled differently.

'At the moment, I have no specific career plan in mind as I am undecided about which discipline I want to go into. My current thought process is to look at job availability and take it from there. Some placements can lead to permanent jobs upon graduation, so hopefully that will work out for me too. In ten years' time, I am just hoping to be happy, healthy with a good work/life balance, feeling confident in my ability as a vet in a team and being in a work setting that works for me.

'My main tip for aspiring vets is to get as much work experience as you can in a variety of disciplines. You have to study them all and work with all species at some point in vet school, so it helps to have a base of knowledge. Also, seeing lots of practice helps you to decide if you really want to do this. It's a tough slog but it can really be worth it. I went back to see practice when I suspended my studies for nine months. I wasn't sure I wanted to carry on with the course at one point, but seeing practice reminded me why I chose veterinary medicine in the first place and that while I may not enjoy all aspects of the degree I knew I would definitely enjoy the end result.

'I would also say, if you can take a year out before heading to university, you should do it! Use it to strengthen your application by doing some long-term placements or getting a job working with animals in some way. Maybe apply to be an assistant at local vet practices or work at a kennels. Gaining life experience before university is so beneficial, and earning some money before first year will make life a lot easier – your student loan never gets you as far as you'd hope!'

Fact: On average, dogs have better – although not as colourful – eyesight than humans.

2 | Horses for courses
Studying veterinary medicine

Given the competitive nature of entry into veterinary school, the idea that there is an element of choice may seem strange. Even when a candidate is fortunate enough to get two or three offers and has to express a preference, the eventual decision can be based on things such as recommendations from family members, friends or the local vet, or whether or not the candidate liked the school or its location on the open day.

Maybe decisions should be based on more objective data than this, but they seldom are. This might not be a bad thing, as decisions made this way often work out quite well. However, although the courses are not vastly different, it is surely sensible for the candidate to be aware of the typical course structure and what is involved. This could be useful at interview. Most importantly, a knowledge of some of the differences between courses could play a part in your decision, should you get two or more offers.

All the courses leading to a degree in veterinary science have to comply with the requirements of the Royal College of Veterinary Surgeons (RCVS) for recognition under the Veterinary Surgeons Act 1966. This is necessary if the degree is to gain the holder admission to the register, which confers the legal right to practise veterinary surgery. It follows that the courses are fundamentally similar; most of the slight differences come towards the clinical end of the degree. This is quite a contrast to many other degrees, where the differences can be much more marked.

Veterinary courses have a carefully structured and integrated programme with one stage leading logically to the next. This logic is not always apparent to the student, who may feel surprised at the amount of theoretical work in the early pre-clinical stage. Later, as you get into the para-clinical and clinical stages, it all begins to make sense. As one final year student commented: 'It's not until the fourth or fifth year that you suddenly realise "So that's why we did that!" ' In this example, the student was talking about the Molecules in Medical Science first year module, leading into the Mechanisms of Drug Action in the second year, and then the administering of these drugs in the clinical years.

The pre-clinical stage

The first two years are pre-clinical and include a lot of lectures, practicals and tutorials. The normal healthy animal is studied. A basic knowledge of the structure and function of the animal body is essential to an understanding of both health and disease. The scientific foundations are being laid with an integrated study of anatomy and physiology. This study of veterinary biological science is augmented by biochemistry, genetics and animal breeding, as well as some aspects of animal husbandry.

Veterinary anatomy

This deals with the structure of the bodies of animals. It includes: the anatomy of locomotion; cellular structure; the development of the body from egg to newborn animal; the study of body tissues such as muscle and bone; and the study of whole organs and systems such as the respiratory and digestive systems. Studying this subject involves anatomical examination of live animals with due emphasis on functional and clinical anatomy. Students spend a lot of their time examining the macroscopic and microscopic structures of the body and its tissue components. One student said: 'We seemed to look through microscopes for hours at various organs and tissues. At the time it was not easy to see the relevance, but later what we had been doing began to make a lot of sense.' There is not only detailed microscopic study of histological sections but also the study of electron micrographs of the cells that make up the different tissues.

Veterinary physiology and biochemistry

This examines how the organs of an animal's body work and their relationship to each other. This is an integral part of the first two years of the course. It is concerned with how the body's control systems work, e.g. temperature regulation, body fluids, and the nervous and cardiovascular systems. You can expect that your studies will include cellular metabolism, renal and alimentary physiology, endocrinology and reproduction.

Animal husbandry

This extends throughout most courses and introduces the student to various farm livestock and related aspects of animal industries. The kind of performance expected from the different species and their respective reproductive capacities are investigated. Livestock nutrition and housing are studied, together with breeding and management. Students learn about the husbandry of domestic animals and some exotic species. Animal husbandry also involves animal handling techniques. These are important skills for the future veterinary surgeon since the patients will often be less co-operative than those met by their medical counterparts. They may even be much more aggressive than humans!

The para-clinical stage

This is sometimes referred to as the second stage. It follows on from the first two years in which normal, healthy animals are studied. Now it is time to undertake studies of disease, the various hereditary and environmental factors responsible, and its treatment. The third year usually sees the study of veterinary pathology introduced (although it sometimes begins in the second year), with parasitology and pharmacology.

Veterinary pathology

This is the scientific study of the causes and nature of various disease processes. This subject is concerned with understanding the structural and functional changes that occur in cells, tissues and organs when there is disease present.

Veterinary parasitology and microbiology

This deals with the multicellular organisms, small and large, that cause diseases, and with bacteria, fungi and viruses. All the basic aspects of parasites of veterinary importance are studied. Students also take courses in applied immunology (the body's natural defences).

Veterinary pharmacology

This is the study of the changes produced in animals by drugs (artificial defences against disease). It comprises several different disciplines including pharmacodynamics (the study of the mechanism of the action of drugs and how they affect the body), pharmacokinetics (absorption, distribution, metabolism and excretion of drugs) and therapeutics (the use of drugs in the prevention and treatment of disease). Some schools introduce this subject in the fourth year.

The clinical or final stage

The last two years of study build on the earlier years, with food hygiene being introduced, while the study of pharmacology is deepened. The meaning of the phrase 'integrated course' now becomes apparent as all the disciplines come together. Medicine, surgery and the diseases of reproduction are taught by clinical specialists in the final stages of the course, and this part of the course is largely practical. More time is spent at the school's veterinary field station. In some cases you can expect to live at the field station in your final year. Much of the study will be in small groups.

You will be allowed to pursue particular interests; however, the main focus will be on the prevention, diagnosis and treatment, by medical or surgical means, of disease and injury in a wide range of species.

Some practical skills learned in the clinical stage

There are many important practical skills that students have to learn in the final clinical period. One of these is the ability to examine the contents of the abdomen through the wall of the rectum without harming or causing infection to the animal through carelessness. You might also learn to use an ultrasound probe to examine, for example, the ovaries. Another use of ultrasound is to listen to the blood flow and the foetal heart sounds in a pregnant sow. Ultrasound can also assist in carrying out an examination of a horse's fetlock.

Students, like the vets they hope to become, can be called out in the middle of the night to a difficult calving. If a cow cannot give birth naturally, the student can help with a Caesarean operation. Using a local anaesthetic allows the operation to take place with the cow standing, which makes the process easier to manage. Practical skill is also important with foaling. It is best if foaling takes place quickly because it is less stressful for the foal, and students are taught that all that is needed is a gentle but firm pull. Final-year students can assist with lambing, and even with the birth of twin lambs. There are many other examples, too numerous to mention.

General anaesthetic can be used for anything from the full range of horse treatments to vasectomising a ram. Many other techniques are also taught: for example, students might look at images of the nasal passages of a horse and see the nasal discharge from a guttural pouch infection. Another example is learning the right way to trim a cow's foot. All animals (that have them!) can suffer problems with their legs or feet. The experienced veterinary surgeon has to have the skill and confidence to be able to remove a cyst from a sheep's brain without causing a rupture.

No wonder, then, that at this final clinical stage students find that all the earlier preparation comes together and makes sense as clinical problem after problem requires you to think and reason from basic scientific principles. Examples such as these do convey the varied nature of the veterinary surgeon's work, but it is as well to remember that in addition to the physician side of the job there is a lot of routine 'dirty' work. Students have, for example, to help maintain cleanliness in the stables and enclosures of the field station. In due course, when you become a working vet, you may at some stage have to tramp round a muddy farmyard on a cold, wet day carrying out blood tests on hundreds of cattle.

Remember that this summary of some of the clinical work encountered on the course is far from comprehensive and should not lead students to believe that this corresponds to a job description.

Extramural rotation (EMR/EMS)

This is sometimes called EMS (Extramural Studies) or 'seeing practice' and the time is divided between farming work and experience in veterinary practice. Students are required during the first two years to complete 10 to 12 weeks of livestock husbandry, depending on which school they attend. Students usually arrange this experience themselves during their holidays, and on the whole they do not seem to have too much difficulty finding a place. Veterinary schools have lists of contacts in their own area with whom you can get in touch. Details of EMS contacts and provisions at each school can be found on the RCVS website (www.rcvs.org.uk/lifelong-learning/students/veterinary-students/extra-mural-studies-ems).

During the third, fourth and final years of their course, students must complete approximately 26 weeks of seeing practice. This will be mainly with veterinary surgeons in mixed general practice, with much shorter periods in, for example, laboratory diagnostic procedures and one or two weeks in an abattoir. Casebooks have to be kept and presented at the final examination.

Some schools, such as the RVC, offer intramural placements. These placements take place within the context of the university across a broad range of practices and other partner organisations.

Notes on veterinary courses in the UK

Aberystwyth

In collaboration with the Royal Veterinary College in London, Aberystwyth has set up a veterinary school in Wales, with the first cohort being welcomed in 2021. The Penglais Campus is home to the Veterinary Education Centre, which has specialist facilities, such as anatomy and clinical skills teaching spaces and companion animal handling training rooms. The first two years are based in Aberystwyth and the final three years are based at RVC's Hawkshead Campus in Hertfordshire, where RVC's exceptional facilities will be used to develop clinical skills.

At Aberystwyth, there are teaching strands that allow modules to be revisited on multiple occasions. These include scientific principles, locomotor, cardiovascular and respiratory, urogenital – renal and reproductive, alimentary, neurology, lymphoreticular and haematopoietic, skin evidence-based medicine and public health. The focus will initially be on healthy animals before then considering disease in different systems and how they are investigated and managed. In the final two years, the majority of teaching is clinically based with participation in intramural and EMS rotations, as well as undertaking a research project.

Assessment: Assessment will consist of both written exams and coursework, involving unseen examinations (essays, multiple-choice questions, short-answer questions) and assignments (essays, projects, practical reports, posters and presentations).

Resits: Aberystwyth's admissions policy states that resits are accepted at GCSE and A level or equivalent without penalty. However, entry requirements must be met in the second sitting. For A level resit candidates, BBC must have been achieved at first sitting, with a B in Biology.

Accreditation: Aberystwyth is working closely with the Royal College of Veterinary Surgeons to ensure that the programme is on track for full accreditation. Accreditation will not be granted until the first cohort have graduated in 2026.

Clinical training: Clinical training will involve Animal Husbandry EMS in the first two years of the course in order to consolidate theoretical learning, improve animal handling and develop knowledge about industry. This will account for 12 weeks in total, including 6 weeks in Wales.

EMS: During the final three years, 26 weeks of clinical EMS will be undertaken to gain experience in clinical- and veterinary-related organisations; 13 of these weeks will be undertaken in Wales. In the final two years, there will be intramural placements within the RVC hospitals.

Bristol

A new spiral curriculum based on an integrated structure focuses on the function of healthy animals, followed by looking at the mechanisms of disease and their clinical management. Vertical themes that run concurrently throughout the course will develop students' understanding of the importance of professional skills, animal health and welfare, and veterinary public health. By being hands-on with animals from year one, practical skills are developed throughout the entire degree programme.

Students are based in Bristol for the first three years of the course, with at least one day per week spent at Langford, where students will be for the last two years. Some units in years one, two and three are taught by pre-clinical departments that are also responsible for teaching science, medical and dental students. This encourages cross-fertilisation of ideas and access to the latest research findings in other scientific fields. The final year is a lecture-free, clinical year for students to practically develop their training.

Assessment: Mainly by examination, written and computer-based, as well as coursework and oral presentations, normally in January and June each year. Additionally, students are also assessed in DSE (directed self-education) and in practical contributions such as the clinical rotations.

Resits: There is usually a chance to resit all or part of the examination in September if the required standard is not reached in June.

Intercalation: Students may interrupt their studies in year three or four to have a chance to intercalate in a science subject that they have studied, in order to obtain an honours BSc.

Clinical training: The clinical part of the veterinary school is at Langford in the Mendip Hills, about 14 miles outside Bristol. The site hosts a wide range of small-animal, equine and farm facilities including first-opinion practices and referral hospitals. There is also a veterinary laboratories agency and abattoir on site. Students may be placed with leading local practices and farms during their lecture-free final year. The emphasis is very much on small-group clinical rotations. You will undertake 12 weeks of pre-clinical extramural practical experience with animals. These placements are undertaken on farms and other animal units, such as kennels and stables, during the holidays of years one and two. A further 26 weeks of clinical extramural studies (EMS) are undertaken during the holidays of the last three years of the programme. For the most part, the clinical study comprises placements in veterinary practice, but it also includes attendance at an abattoir and optional research placements.

EMS: Bristol is set apart from the other universities as for part of their clinical EMS all students have a 'Foster Practice'. The guidelines recommend that students take 10 to 14 weeks at this practice over the three-year clinical period, so they gain continuous experience. As they say, 'our evidence shows that over the three years they develop in knowledge, skills and confidence. Practitioners and students become familiar with each other, opening greater opportunities for the students to learn and to contribute to the practice.' The type of Foster Practice you will attend, which you choose in your second year, will be based on the variety of experience available to you at your chosen practice, as it is especially important to gain as varied an experience as possible. The rest of your CEMS (Clinical Extramural Studies) is up to you, though you have to work within limits: namely, you can only spend up to 10 weeks overseas and six weeks undertaking research. You receive plenty of extra support from the EMS administration office and will be expected to detail this support in the RCVS Student Experience Log when giving your reflections on EMS.

Cambridge

This is the smallest of the veterinary schools. One of its principal strengths is the extensive use the course makes of practical teaching.

The course extends for six years and is divided equally between the pre-clinical and clinical parts. The first three years of the course cover the scientific basis of veterinary medicine in lectures and small-group supervisions; you can expect 20–25 hours of teaching per week. The initial two years are concerned with the basic medical and veterinary sciences, between which there is much common ground at this early stage, bringing you into contact with students from other disciplines. There are also more applied courses in farm-animal husbandry and preparing for the veterinary profession. For the third year, you can elect to study in depth a subject of your own choice from a wide range of options, leading to the award of the BA (Hons) degree at the end of year three. The flexibility of the tripos system is one of its most attractive features. The tripos system is a system in two parts whereby you need to complete both parts in order to achieve an honours degree at Cambridge. Cambridge was the first university to introduce a lecture-free, clinical final year where students work in practice.

There are state-of-the-art facilities on site and there is one of the leading cancer units in Europe, capable of delivering radiotherapy to all sizes of animal. Equally, there is a Clinical Skills Centre with interactive models and simulators that students are encouraged to make use of during their course.

During your pre-clinical studies, students must complete a minimum of 12 weeks of EMS during university vacations.

Assessment: Examinations in the Easter and Summer terms, depending on the year of study, with your progress being reviewed weekly in subject supervisions. Assessment is a mixture of essays, short answers, multiple-choice questions and practical examinations.

Resits: There is an opportunity to resit veterinary examinations in September.

Intercalation: An intercalated degree will be awarded to all veterinary students (not affiliate students). Approximately three years after being awarded, this will be upgraded to a master's degree.

Clinical training: The clinical training course is taught in the Department of Veterinary Medicine at the West Cambridge Campus. The emphasis is on small-group practical teaching, often eight students in a group, in rotations (or three to four students in some final year rotations). The fourth and fifth years' studies include microbiology, pathology, medicine and surgery. The final year is lecture free with hands-on experience and a period of elective study, and is continuously assessed. The farm-animal practice provides first-opinion clinical services to surrounding farms, including the university dairy farm just a few miles away. A farm-animal referral centre was opened in 2002. Advantage is also taken of the Queen's Veterinary School Hospital (a referral hospital with a full range of modern surgical and medical suites), a nearby Royal Society for the Prevention of Cruelty to Animals (RSPCA) first-opinion clinic, specialist equine practices in and around Newmarket and the Animal Health Trust. The department has its own first-opinion practice, an equine referral hospital and equine surgery facilities. During your clinical training, you must complete at least 26 weeks of clinical extramural study during university vacations.

Opportunities for research ensure that veterinary teaching is embedded in the latest cutting-edge discoveries. At the end of the course, those graduating will receive the VetMB membership to the RCVS.

EMS: In the Department of Clinical Veterinary Medicine there is a database of practices that accept Cambridge students and participate in Cambridge's EMS assessment procedure. From this database, students select where they would like to go – they equally have the choice of the National EMS database – and then discuss this with their Veterinary School Clinical Supervisor or the EMS Co-ordinator; the key is balance and variety, all the time remembering that as well as developing your skills, you also have to comply with the national requirement. The expectation is that you spend at least 18 weeks at private veterinary practices within the UK, to include a minimum core requirement of: six weeks' small animal, six weeks' farm animal and two weeks' equine experience.

Edinburgh

Established in 1823, the Royal (Dick) School of Veterinary Studies was the second veterinary school to be established in the UK and the first in Scotland. The 'Dick' school benefits from a collegial community alongside up-to-date techniques. As Edinburgh has American Veterinary Medical Association (AVMA) accreditation, as well as the European Association of Establishments for Veterinary Education (EAEVE), the veterinary degree course (Bachelor of Veterinary Medicine and Surgery or BVMS) gives undergraduate students the opportunity to apply their skills in different countries in the future, whether as a vet or in biomedical research, for example. Edinburgh is internationally recognised for its commitment to excellence through a strong base of research and teaching in a well-supported learning environment. The Easter Bush Campus incorporates a new, purpose-built £40 million teaching building, small-animal, equine and farm-animal hospital facilities with both first-opinion and referral services, and the world-renowned Roslin Institute, located in a new £60 million facility offering opportunities to carry out research supervised by pre-eminent researchers in numerous fields.

As a student, you will also study at Langhill, which is the university's 250-hectare livestock farm. At Langhill, students will learn about animal handling and farm animal medicine. There is also a unique Exotic Animals and Wildlife Service for first-hand experience of dealing with both exotic pets and wildlife commonly found in the UK.

As a result of Colorado State University's status internationally, there is an opportunity for students to study abroad here also.

Assessment: Professional examinations usually include a mix of written and practical components with contributions from in-course assessment, continuous assessment or project work.

Resits: There is an opportunity to resit degree examinations in August if the required standards are not met during the year.

Intercalation: Students with a special interest in animal disease can choose to interrupt their studies and complete a BSc (Hons) in Veterinary Science, usually after year two or three of the programme, which involves one year of advanced study in many different areas including: biochemistry, neuroscience, veterinary biomedical sciences or microbiology and infection. For exceptional students, there is the opportunity to study a one-year research MSc or an intercalated three-year PhD. Students can also enrol on one of the school's prestigious taught MSc programmes, which include Animal Welfare and Behaviour, Infectious Diseases, Conservation Medicine, Equine Science and One Health.

Clinical training: This begins at the start of the first year in the clinically integrated programme with training in examining normal animals across the common species, progressing to abnormal animals in later years. The lecture-free final year emphasises small-group practical, clinical experience where students undertake clinical rotations in the school's hospitals and support services, giving students practical experience in a wide range of disciplines. The final year is longer than the previous years and incorporates an externship and elective periods to allow focus on areas of individual interest. Students also produce a personal and professional development portfolio, which enhances their employability, encourages lifelong learning and promotes professionalism.

EMS: The first stage of EMS learning at Edinburgh involves undertaking six weeks of Observational EMS. You will be welcome to start the clinical EMS at any time once you have completed your pre-clinical animal health EMS. This means you will likely be doing Observational EMS between the second and third years in order to experience how a vet practice works as a business. You are expected to be clinically aware by the third year, even though you will have received no training. You then undertake Practical EMS for 20 weeks, for which you can tailor the experience to your interests and career roles, while being realistic in setting objectives and not placing too many demands on practitioners. You will have to complete a portfolio to comply with 'RCVS Day One Competences'. RCVS Day One Competences is a document that sets out the basic and essential competences and skills required by the time you graduate, to ensure that you are safe to practise veterinary medicine on day one of your first job.

Glasgow

Founded in 1862, this is one of the larger schools. It is located at Garscube, four miles to the north-west of Glasgow. The school is considered to be the top in Scotland and the top in the UK, so you will be taught by world-leading professionals. On the site are the pre-clinical and clinical departments, as well as the Weipers Centre for Equine Welfare and a small-animal hospital, and nearby is Cochno Farm and Research Centre, which is used by the university as an additional teaching facility. Some pre-clinical teaching is conducted at the main university campus near the city centre, which enables students to benefit from the opportunities at both sites. The faculty is one of only four veterinary schools in Europe to be accredited to British, European and American standards. In a National Student Survey, Glasgow students reported a 97% satisfaction rating. Delivered in three phases (foundation, clinical and professional) the course follows an integrated structure with vertical themes, placing an emphasis on the skills you will require working as a vet. The final year is a lecture-free year. Glasgow has approved status from the American Veterinary Medical Association (AVMA) and as such, there are plenty of study abroad opportunities.

Assessment: Examination by written and practical work.

Resits: These can take place in September of each year. A second failure may result in repeating a year; normally this is only possible for one year of the course.

Intercalation: At the end of year three, students may study for a one-year BSc (VetSc) honours degree before starting the clinical training. Eight subjects are available. A two-year intercalated BSc honours degree at the end of either year two or year three is another possibility.

Clinical training: The lecture-free final year maximises the opportunities for small-group clinical teaching around domestic animal cases. This takes place at the faculty's busy referral hospital and through EMS undertaken in practices and other veterinary institutions in the UK and overseas.

Special features: As with all UK veterinary schools, every student is expected to complete 38 weeks of EMS in holiday periods. In the first two years students are expected to complete 12 weeks of EMS in the holidays. In the third, fourth and fifth year holiday periods, you are expected to complete 26 weeks of EMS. On the intercalated degree programme students who are in their second or third years of the Bachelor of Veterinary Medicine and Surgery (BVMS) course can elect to come out of the degree and study for an additional qualification on top for one or two years, before re-entering the BVMS programme.

EMS: You are expected to fulfil the 12 weeks' pre-clinical EMS with domestic animal, lambing and dairy farming, as well as six weeks' equine care. After that, your 26 weeks' clinical EMS will start with six weeks' preparatory work. You are advised to experience at least three different types of veterinary work for overall variety to develop your skills and understanding. The remaining time will be Practical EMS of 20 weeks, and this takes place in your latter clinical years. Importantly, you are given flexibility to choose EMS based on what you are interested in and, equally, it will be your responsibility to gain 'RCVS Day One Competences' across a range of species.

Harper & Keele

Harper & Keele Veterinary School is newly formed and combines the extensive resources of both Harper Adams' outstanding reputation as an animal sciences provider and Keele's world-renowned laboratory facilities. The five-year course has a strong practical focus, with clinical experience from year one. They utilise a spiral curriculum to incorporate important theoretical knowledge into relevant clinical contexts. The programme being delivered is intense, with around 28 contact hours per week. Students will be split equally across both university sites, which are 23 miles (50 minutes) apart, with any lectures occurring being live-streamed to the alternative campus. Students should expect to travel to the other site occasionally to make use of the relevant facilities, and a shuttle bus service will be provided for transport between them.

Assessment: Assessment will involve clinical skills assessment modules which are based upon demonstrating practical competencies, each of which must be passed. There is a progressive development of the modules covered within each year, with the relevant assessments increasing in difficulty with each year. Assessments in the fifth year are based on clinical rotations.

Resits: A level resit candidates are considered providing there is no more than one resit in each subject. If students are unsuccessful during an admissions cycle, they will be reconsidered in following cycles.

Accreditation: The Royal College of Veterinary Surgeons is working closely with both Keele and Harper Adams to ensure that the new degree meets the standards for accreditation and that graduates will be eligible for registration. Formal accreditation cannot be granted until 2025, once its first set of students have graduated.

Clinical training: Clinical training occurs throughout the degree at workplace-based placements with practice partners of the universities.

EMS: EMS are taken throughout the degree as an essential part of veterinary education and during the early years, they are student led. EMS placements can be arranged anywhere in the country, but final-year placements will be managed by the veterinary school and will therefore be within travelling distance from the host site.

Liverpool

This was the first veterinary school to be incorporated into a university structure and therefore the first to establish a university-certified veterinary degree. The Faculty of Veterinary Science celebrated its centenary in 2004. In 2020 it had a 93% student satisfaction rating according to figures from the National Student Survey (NSS). The principal degree course leading to the Bachelor of Veterinary Science (BVSc) MRCVS, the D100, is a five-year course and students also have the opportunity to incorporate an intercalated BSc. The options for intercalating include a BSc in Conservation Medicine and an MSc in Veterinary Infectious Disease and Control. These courses are also offered to students from other veterinary schools. The faculty also offers a three-year BSc (Hons) in Bioveterinary Science. Teaching on this course is shared between the Faculty of Veterinary Science and the School of Biological Sciences.

Veterinary students spend the first three years of the course on campus in Liverpool studying pre-clinical and para-clinical subjects. The course is modularised. During the fourth and final years, the students are based at Leahurst, the teaching hospital on the Wirral peninsula 18 miles away, which has facilities for equine and livestock cases and a small-animal hospital. First-opinion work (dealing with calls from clients) is undertaken at Fern Grove practice in Liverpool. There are two separate practices operating out of Leahurst, serving the large local equine population and the agricultural sector, and they also get referrals from all over northern England for horses with colic, skin tumours and orthopaedic conditions. Farm visits and investigations extend to the sheep farming areas of north Wales and the dairy farms of Cheshire and Lancashire. Leahurst is in close proximity to Chester Zoo and there is a strong interest in wildlife diseases and animal behaviour.

The university has also established a Foundation to Health and Veterinary Studies Programme (Year 0) with local FE (further education) partners as an access course for those wishing to study a five-year veterinary course, which is typically aimed at mature students and those who have taken a gap away from their studies. You should refer directly to the website for further details.

Assessment: Examination is by both examination and, latterly, practical.

Resits: Resit applications are encouraged.

Intercalation: The veterinary sciences course can be taken with or without an intercalated year.

Clinical training: There is substantial practical work throughout the course; 26 weeks of EMS are completed between years three and five.

EMS: Your first two years include undertaking 12 weeks of pre-clinical animal husbandry EMS. As clinical skills have been introduced into year one, there is an expectation for you to gain some clinical EMS in the first two years of the course. This experience will provide early exposure to the running of veterinary practices as businesses. You then have a requirement of compulsory and choice EMS.

Compulsory PCEMS (Pre-clinical EMS): lambing, dairy, cattle, horses, pigs, dogs/cats, poultry (one week each).

Compulsory CEMS: public health (two weeks), small animal, farm animal, equine (three weeks each).

Arranging the placements is the responsibility of the student and you must adhere to the EMS requirements. You need to identify and detail your 'learning objectives' before undertaking these placements and then discuss with your EMS placement supervisor.

London

The Royal Veterinary College (RVC), based in Camden Town and Hertfordshire, is the oldest (established in 1791) and largest of the eight UK veterinary schools and the only veterinary school worldwide to be fully accredited by both European (EAEVE) and US (AVMA) authorities, alongside full accreditation with the RCVS and the Australasian Veterinary Board Council (AVBC). This allows graduates to practise in other countries. As one of the University of London's 19 self-governing colleges, the RVC is the UK's only independent veterinary school and it also has a Centre for Excellence in Teaching and Learning. The RVC has developed innovative approaches to learning, and students are equipped with the knowledge and skills needed to succeed throughout their working life. Students spend their first two years undertaking comprehensive pre-clinical studies at the Camden Campus, and then proceed to clinical studies at the Hawkshead Campus in Hertfordshire (north of London).

Assessment: The college uses a wide variety of assessment methods, teaching from a comparative perspective. Some of them are highly innovative and have been pioneered by the RVC. Emphasis is placed on practical work and students are tested by clinical examinations (Objective Structured Clinical Examinations: OSCE), Directly Observed Procedural Skills (DOPS), oral examinations and spot tests as well as written examinations, including multiple-choice questions (MCQs) and extended multiple-choice questions (EMQs), problem-solving questions and essay questions.

Resits: A level resits are considered, providing the student achieves the highest possible grade in the second sitting. Resits are also permitted during the course; students are required to pass overall to progress.

Intercalation: Students may intercalate a BSc after successful completion of, normally, the second year. Students can also be considered for certain BSc courses offered by University of London colleges or other universities, or for the RVC's own veterinary comparative pathology course.

Clinical training: In year three, students begin their clinical EMS at a variety of veterinary placements, eventually totalling 26 weeks (up to six of these weeks can be overseas) by the middle of year four. Lectures are timetabled early in the week. On Fridays students get the opportunity to get feedback on their knowledge using the computer-based MCQs. The tutorial system has been revamped recently and students take part in monthly groups of six to eight students. Most of the remaining time is spent gaining hands-on experience in RVC clinics and hospitals (intramural rotations). During year four, students also spend at least eight weeks devising and executing a research project on any aspect of veterinary science that interests them. In holiday periods, there is an expectation for students to complete 12 weeks of placements.

EMS: In order to complete the 26 weeks of CEMS, you are expected to undertake 10 weeks of EMS before clinical rotations start in the second term of the fourth year, with the remaining 16 weeks taking place during clinical rotation. In the first phase, you should see this as preparation work to give you the chance to see how practices really work. The amount of actual hands-on time is limited because clinical skills will not have been learnt yet, but this should be seen as time to understand how a practice operates as a business. In the first period of EMS, students will have to spend at least six weeks at 'three different multi-vet first opinion practices' in the UK, preferably three lots of two-week blocks. You will be encouraged to return to these places during your degree course to further develop your knowledge. The further 20 weeks of your EMS should be used to develop a variety of skills with different animal species. The ideal will be to gain at least two weeks' practical experience with small animals, two weeks in an equine practice, and two weeks in a large animal practice (these should be busy practices to experience working under pressure). The RCVS requires all graduates to be 'a "species omnicompetent" veterinarian regardless of their personal species preferences or future career plans.' RVC students are to attend placements for at least two weeks as it gives more detailed learning; one-week placements are not permitted in the third year. All experience should be made in consultation with your clinical tutor.

Nottingham

Based at the university's Sutton Bonington Campus, Nottingham's School of Veterinary Medicine and Science accepted its first students in 2006. It aims to equip students with all the necessary diagnostic, medical and surgical skills. In 2020, the university was ranked sixth (see

Table 2 on page 51), with 82% in student satisfaction ratings and 98% in graduate employment for veterinary medicine. Its course integrates clinical medicine and surgery with pathology and basic sciences, to ensure that its graduates gain the best possible foundations for a career in the veterinary profession. Studies include time spent at the new, purpose-built clinical teaching facilities and with local clinical practitioners. The five-year degree course leads students from day one through a clinically integrated curriculum and problem-based approach providing learning in all aspects of veterinary medicine and surgery. In years one and two, students undertake a minimum of 12 weeks' animal husbandry EMS, and at least four weeks of clinical EMS in year two. All students undertake a research project in year three, and a minimum of 12 weeks of clinical EMS in both year three and year four. At the end of year three, students graduate with a Bachelor of Veterinary Medical Sciences (BVMedSci). In year four, students will become more accustomed to the business and entrepreneurial skills that are necessary in local practice. The summer term of year four and the whole final year are spent in clinical rotations. This includes a minimum of 10 weeks' EMS. Another 25 weeks of intramural rotations are undertaken in year five, which is lecture free. Intramural rotations may include time at both large- and small-animal practices, laboratory facilities and specialist facilities. After five years of successful study the degrees of Bachelor of Veterinary Medicine (BVM) and Bachelor of Veterinary Surgery (BVS) are awarded.

In addition to the D100 course, there is a D101 course, which includes a preliminary year for those who need to further their knowledge, and a D190 course that includes a gateway year designed for those who need to acquire the scientific knowledge necessary for the profession. You should refer directly to the website for further details.

Assessment: Using different types of assessment, Nottingham aims to measure a wide variety of skill- and knowledge-based learning objectives. There are in-course module examinations including practical tests, essays and short projects. There are also informal assessment opportunities for students to evaluate their progress.

Resits: Applicants will be considered if they resit A levels, though they do not accept students who have started a university course elsewhere (i.e. if they have started an alternative BSc without finishing it). Resits during the course are available.

Intercalation: It can be possible to integrate a master's degree into the course.

Clinical training: Each student undergoes as standard 12 weeks of EMS in animal husbandry and 26 weeks overall of EMS in a clinical environment.

EMS: Once pre-clinical EMS has been completed, students undertake a programme of Clinical Extramural Studies (CEMS), which is structured as 20 weeks' student-organised CEMS and six weeks' Vet School-organised 'Formalised CEMS'. This usually starts around the end of year two but until the end of Easter in year three, students can only undergo a maximum of six weeks so that students gain experiences still whilst realising the need to continue developing their clinical skills. The emphasis for what placements students should take and where is placed on the students, empowering them and forcing them to take charge of their studies; however, they will have access to a database and a support network to help them. They will be allocated a clinical tutor and will need to produce an action plan for every placement and make use of the Clinical EMS Handbook given to them during their second year and talks from in-house tutors on getting the most out of CEMS. Placements can be chosen from the database of practices in the Placements Office, along with the RCVS Directory of Veterinary Practices.

Surrey

Based in Guildford, the University of Surrey's is the newest veterinary school and is currently developing year on year. In 2015, a new state-of-the-art, purpose-built School of Veterinary Medicine opened which has plentiful teaching space and includes a world-class veterinary Clinical Skills Centre. The school offers a research-led degree, which provides an interactive environment for learning. More interesting is that the five-year course is designed to create collaborations in animal and human health, with hands-on practical experience from the outset. There is a mixture of taught, clinical and practical work which enables students to fully engage with the material. The School of Veterinary Medicine aims to work alongside chosen veterinary practices to provide students with outstanding experience in general practice and the clinical training required.

A unique aspect of the university is that the veterinary school is currently working with Calgary, Wisconsin, North Carolina and São Paulo Universities as part of the University Global Partnership Network (UGPN). It also works closely with various associations, notably the AHVLA (Animal Health and Veterinary Laboratories Agency), giving the opportunity to develop skills in different areas, such as surveillance, risk analysis and policy.

In accordance with RCVS policy, all students must have 12 weeks of animal husbandry EMS in Years 1 and 2, and 26 weeks of EMS over the following years. There will be a total of 32 weeks of intramural rotations in the clinical year of the course in a wide variety of areas: small-animal practice, surgery, emergency and critical care, veterinary public health, pathology, production animals, equine and electives.

Assessment: The curriculum is arranged to focus on different body systems and integrated horizontally to cover a wide range of subject areas. All aspects of the course are assessed with a range of formative assessments to aid students' work, a portfolio and a skills diary. Formal assessments require all modules to be passed to progress each year.

Resits: Applicants with resits are considered and also those who have applied once before but did not get an interview. However, the school will not consider those who were unsuccessful at interview first time.

Accreditation: In January 2020, a Recognition Order for the University of Surrey's veterinary degree was approved, meaning that it is now formally accredited.

Clinical training: Students will undertake core clinical rotations as part of the clinically integrated veterinary medicine and science degree. They will also be able to choose from bespoke options to gain unique training in specialist areas, including an option for a research project.

EMS: All students will undertake a minimum of 12 weeks of Animal Husbandry Extramural Studies (AHEMS) in years one and two and 26 weeks of Extramural Studies (EMS) after that, in accordance with the RCVS guidelines.

> Reminder: EMS requirement. To meet RCVS requirements, all students at all veterinary schools must complete 12 weeks of pre-clinical and 26 weeks of clinical EMS, prior to taking their final examinations.

> Fact: Cows can sleep standing up, but they can only dream lying down.

3 | Separating the sheep from the goats

Preparation and experience

Wanting to become a veterinary surgeon is a long-term commitment. It requires perseverance and a lot of determination. If all goes well and you get the results demanded by all the veterinary schools, it will still take a further five or six years to qualify. Many students facing the intensive study required in the sixth form will find it hard to look further ahead than the next test or practical; yet much more than this is needed if you are to stand a chance of getting into veterinary school.

Starting early

Ideally, the pursuit of your interest in animals and their welfare – in short, your commitment – should have started much earlier than sixth form. There are numerous cases of aspiring vets who have begun their enquiries as early as the age of 12, and certainly many have started gaining their practical experience by the age of 14.

Some vets grew up on a farm and knew that they wanted this kind of life. Others come from an urban background and have developed an interest despite not being brought up in an animal-friendly environment. This interest can be kick-started in a variety of ways and can develop through, for instance, pet ownership, the Herriot books, one of the numerous television programmes such as *Animal Park*, *Super Vets* and *Vet Safari*, or the influence of a friend. 'It's a great life, there's so much variety,' was one student's view. 'You realise it when you start going out getting experience. You see that you can be a vet in a town or in the countryside, that some practices are much larger than others and that some are very busy while others appear more relaxed.'

One young vet said that she had begun her enquiries at about the age of 14 and started working at weekends – her experience began with work in a stables where she began to learn horse riding. Another recalled how she had done kennel work at weekends for four years before becoming a veterinary student. It goes without saying that cleaning out kennels is a dirty, often unpleasant job, and to do this over such a long period shows an impressive degree of commitment and dedication from an early age. Some students have the chance to gain early experience on a nearby farm. But what would you do there? One farmer's wife commented: 'We would expect a 14-year-old to help feed the livestock, to help with bedding-up, which means putting fresh straw in the pens, and sweeping up.' You should be alert to what is happening around you and ask questions: 'Why is that calf coughing? What are you giving it?'

Of course, not everyone comes to this decision early in life, and if you haven't amassed years of work experience by the time you reach sixth form, it is still possible to submit a successful application. That being said, the work experience requirements for each vet school in the UK are quite considerable, so you will need to be highly organised in arranging experience to ensure that the minimum requirements are met.

Getting more experience

As those pre-A level years unfold, it makes sound sense to follow up your visits to the local stables, kennels or farm with a week or two spent with your local vet. The point is that you are not just trying to find ways to satisfy the admissions tutor at veterinary school who may one day read an application that you have completed, important though that is; you are also testing your own motivation. This is vital because, make no mistake, you are going to need all the focus you can muster. The task you are about to set yourself is going to draw upon all your commitment, dedication and determination.

It should be pointed out that students who are still at school or sixth-form college will be very lucky to find themselves in the consulting room with the vet. This is because anxious owners will not always appreciate or understand the need for someone of school age to be present. It is much more likely that you will be asked to spend time with the veterinary nurses, where you will be able to handle animals and see how you cope with them. The idea is to see how the student reacts to aspects of animal husbandry at an early stage, and to ascertain whether you can deal with cleaning up the blood and faeces that go with animal practice. After an artery has stopped pumping or diarrhoea has ended, there is a clean-up job to be done – this is an early experience for many well-intentioned potential vets. Can you take it?

Confirmation of a period spent at a veterinary establishment is one of the conditions for entry to an undergraduate course leading to the degree of Bachelor of Veterinary Medicine or Science. Without getting out and finding out what it is like to deal with sick animals as well as normal, healthy ones, how will you know that you are suited to a career dedicated to providing a service to animals and their owners? As one student put it: 'Knowing what animals look like doesn't necessarily prepare you for what they feel or smell like. There is only one way to find out and that is to get into close contact.' You may think you love animals because of the way you feel about your own pet, but going from the particular to the general may cause you to think quite differently. You might even be allergic to some animals. You need to be certain that you still feel happy about dealing with animals in general and that you really mean business.

Specific university requirements

Work experience is also vital if you are to have a chance of being called for interview, and without an interview you cannot be offered a place. Some of the veterinary schools are more specific than others about what they expect in the way of practical experience.

- **Aberystwyth** recognises the restrictions in gaining work experience because of Covid-19, and with their first cohort starting the course in 2021, they have asked for 35 hours of work experience in veterinary practice and 35 hours of work experience in non-clinical environments with live animals. Applicants will also be expected to complete RVC's Applicant Supplementary Form.
- **Bristol** has minimum requirements of one week's (35 hours) work experience in a veterinary practice, as well as a further one week's experience in any other animal-related setting. This is a total of 70 hours and Bristol stipulates that it should be completed within three-years prior to the application cycle. Exceeding the requirements won't necessarily put you at an advantage, and having future plans for work experience won't count towards the required 70 hours. Bristol won't typically review the personal statement on the UCAS form, but instead ask applicants to complete the Supplementary Assessment Questionnaire, which comprises two sections: Section A, which enables applicants to declare their work experience, and section B, which asks a series of questions that allows the applicant to show their understanding of the role of the vet. As Bristol does not interview applicants typically, it is crucially important that this form is completed accurately and thoroughly. If students have not met the minimum work experience requirement, they are still able to submit an application, especially in the context of Covid-19, but may be expected to undertake an online virtual work-experience course.
- **Cambridge** does not demand large amounts of veterinary work experience, and advises acquiring around 10 to 12 cumulative days' worth – just enough that you can discuss your experiences at inter-view and to gain a sufficient understanding of what working in the profession entails. They recognise that extensive experience is not accessible to everyone, so impressive or unusual placements do not provide applicants with an advantage. All applications to

Cambridge require completion of the Supplementary Application Questionnaire. If you have not been able to get the required amount of work experience – because of the Covid-19 pandemic or a late decision to pursue veterinary medicine, for example – then this is the place to discuss it.

- **Edinburgh** states that the more broad your work-experience placements, the better, though they do not specify a set number of days or weeks. With the breadth of placements being their main focus, you should aim to gain experience in a range of areas, including large- and small-animal practice, livestock farms and other animal establishments, such as zoos, kennels, stables and catteries. They also encourage abattoir visits and laboratory experience. Generally, Edinburgh will only consider work experience that has been undertaken and not that which has been planned. However, because of the pandemic, Edinburgh will consider any planned work experience that was cancelled due to Covid-19 for 2021 entry. Where applicants have not been able to undertake work experience, they are advised to conduct online research to address any gaps this might have left and they will also consider the completion of online work-experience courses. While the personal statement will be reviewed, applicants to Edinburgh must also submit a Work Experience Summary (WES) form.

- **Glasgow** does not specify any specific requirements for work-experience placements, but encourages applicants to have at least some hands-on experience with farm animals as well as a few days with a veterinary surgeon to ensure that they are familiar with the demands of the course and the career. Undertaking the online virtual work-experience course will also be considered during the pandemic.

- **Harper & Keele** asks for two weeks in veterinary practice, ideally covering both large and small animals, and up to four weeks in non-clinical placements. Applicants will be expected to discuss these placements in detail at interview and in the online reflective form. In the context of Covid-19, minimum requirements for 2021 entry have been removed; however, you may need to provide details of planned but cancelled placements, and you may need to discuss these at interview, including why you chose to pursue them and what you expected to gain from them.

- **Liverpool** encourages applicants to undertake work-experience placements in two of farm, equine and small-animal settings. With Covid-19, applicants for 2021 entry are not expected to have undertaken any work experience beyond March 2020 and, with this in mind, they will interview applicants who have obtained five days' worth of veterinary work experience in any field. So as not to exclude candidates who have missed out on work-experience placements due to the pandemic, they will also accept completion of a virtual work-experience online course in its place. Applicants will need to complete an online questionnaire to state the experience that they have been able to acquire.

- The **RVC** specifies quality work experience over quantity. It has a minimum requirement of two weeks of work experience in a veterinary practice and two weeks in a different animal environment, such as a kennel, cattery, animal shelter, farm, stables, city farm, pet shop, lambing, wildlife park, zoo, etc. You do not have to have gained experience in all these areas. You are encouraged to think creatively and experiences should reflect a good sense of the veterinary role in wider society. All applicants must fill in an online work experience questionnaire to support their application. The RVC also requests references from your work-experience placements, so you are encouraged to obtain these as you go. Due to the ongoing impacts of the Covid-19 pandemic, the RVC are aware that planned placements may be disrupted, and so for 2021 entry they have reduced their requirements to one week (35 hours) in veterinary practice or non-clinical working environments prior to submitting an application, with the 70 hours of experience in practice and non-clinical environments with live animals as outlined above to be acquired by July 2021. If only these minimum requirements have been met, then the remaining work experience placements will be included as part of the conditional offer.

- **Nottingham** asks that its applicants have four weeks' worth of work experience that involves animal handling in a broad range of contexts, such as small-animal husbandry, lambing, small equine, dairy, zoos, stables, rescue centres, kennels, catteries, farms and veterinary practices. Typically, all work experience must be completed prior to the 15 October UCAS deadline, but with Covid-19, applications for 2021 entry will not be negatively affected if applicants have been unable to complete planned work experience by this date after March 2020.

- **Surrey** asks students to have a minimum of four weeks' work experience with animals and this must include one week in a veterinary practice. Alternatively, they will consider one week of experience at an animal-related organisation plus the completion of an online virtual work-experience programme. Work on a farm, in stables, kennels, surgery, research and an abattoir is encouraged. It also requires an official reference from the employer for all work completed prior to the application deadline of 15 October each year, though for 2021 entry, this deadline has been extended to 15 January 2021. To be counted, references must be provided in an official format. Applicants must also complete an online questionnaire shortly after the UCAS deadline where there is an opportunity to demonstrate knowledge and understanding of the veterinary profession and motivation to pursue a career in this area. This will involve a more in-depth work experience discussion, discussion of a topical issue and completion of a Situational Judgement Test (SJT) that will assess knowledge of the Royal College of Veterinary Surgeons Day One Competencies.

Making the initial contact

Making the first contact can be quite difficult, often because of your nerves, inexperience or because the vet is cautious and reluctant to take on an unknown commitment. You need to overcome this as soon as possible, because the most proactive students are the ones that get the best work-experience placements. At the end of the day, the worst anyone can say is no. However, they only want to hear from you, not your parent or guardian. Remember, this is your application, your future and therefore your call to make. It will be seen so much more positively than if your parent calls for you. After the initial approach has been made, the next stage – developing contacts – will seem easy with your growing self-reliance.

Your local vet will know a lot of people through working with animals. A recommendation, or better still an introduction by your local vet to a large-animal practice or a local farmer, may lead to work in a stables or work with sheep, for example. You will get to know people yourself and this will build your confidence.

Developing contacts in this way is known as networking. Taking the initiative like this can do you more favours than always relying on the careers department at your school. However, it is worth checking to see whether your school careers department can help you, as they may have existing contacts, though it is best not to rely solely on this.

Remember that in the end it is your own responsibility to get practical experience. Busy people such as vets and farmers are likely to be more impressed with those who exhibit the confidence and self-reliance to make their own approaches.

What the vet will want

Some vets are reluctant to allow young, inexperienced people into their practice. This is understandable. They know that many people are attracted to the idea of becoming a vet, but in a busy setting it can be difficult to commit to assisting a young person. Though you may be eager to prolong placements, do not be surprised if some vets suggest that you should first visit for just a day. The reason for this is that they feel they need to meet you first before committing themselves, and this will also allow you to identify whether it is an environment that you can see yourself working in.

What will the local vet ask you to do? This will depend on the vet. This may involve three days of blood and gore on farms, or your local vet may be a small practice dealing mainly with companion animals – most often cats and dogs, but also rabbits, goldfish, gerbils and budgies.

Some practices are mixed, dealing with farm animals, horses and pets, while in country areas there are practices that deal mainly with farm animals. The types of practice and their size vary widely. The average practice has three or four vets; however, at the one extreme about 2% have more than 10, each with a degree of specialisation, and at the other end of the scale, about 25% are single-handed practices, requiring practitioners to deal with a wide range of work. This being so, the resources that the vet will be able to draw upon will also vary widely.

Shaping up in the surgery

A head nurse in a medium-sized mixed practice uses the following list of questions to enable her or him to judge how students helping in the small-animal surgery are shaping up. They are all well worth considering to make sure you're fully prepared for work experience.

- How keen are they to help in every area? For example, do they clean up willingly?
- How observant are they? Do they watch how we do the bandaging or how we hold the animal straight ready for an injection? Do they watch carefully how we take a blood sample, administer an anaesthetic or set up an intravenous drip?
- Do they maintain a neat and tidy appearance and clean themselves before going in to see a small-animal client? This is very important to the owner.
- Are they friendly towards the client? Do they make conversation and try to establish a relationship?
- Do they ask questions about what they do not understand? They shouldn't be afraid to ask even while procedures are being carried out.
- Are they listening to what is being said and the way it is being said? Do they appreciate the experience that allows the vet to counsel owners on sensitive issues, for example on reducing their favourite pet's diet? This is not an easy message to get across to an overindulgent owner and a vet needs a good 'bedside manner' to be able to tell the owner what must be done without giving offence.

Checklist of experience

Always take up any opportunities that you are offered. Variety of experience will not only broaden your understanding of the profession you seek to join, but will also impress the admissions tutors when they come to scrutinise your UCAS application. Here are some suggestions. Remember, some applicants to veterinary school will have carried out a few of these suggestions four or five years before applying! Others are applicable only to Year 11 or sixth-form students. But if you can tick every box by the time you submit your form in October of your upper-sixth year, well done!

- Get work experience in catteries and/or boarding kennels.
- Work in the local pet shop.
- Make contact with a local vet and indicate your interest by helping with some of the menial tasks. If you are keen you will not mind doing the dirty work.
- Get at least two to three weeks' experience with a large-animal veterinary practice or occasional days or weekends over a long period. Without this, you will not be accepted into veterinary school, no matter how well-qualified you are academically. You must also gain some experience of working in a companion-animal practice. Some candidates are fortunate in having access to mixed practices in which they can gain familiarity with handling large and small animals.
- Visit a local dairy farm and get acquainted with farm work, which accounts for at least 30% of all veterinary science work. Try also to assist on a sheep farm at lambing time.
- Work with horses at a riding stables. (Riding establishments are subject to inspection by an authorised veterinary surgeon.)
- Visit an abattoir if possible.
- Get in touch with one of the animal charities, such as the People's Dispensary for Sick Animals (PDSA) or the RSPCA, and find out about their work.
- Spend a day in a pharmaceutical laboratory concerned with the drugs used by vets as well as medics, or in a laboratory of the Department for Environment, Food and Rural Affairs (Defra).
- Try for any additional relevant experience that may be within your reach, e.g. at a zoo, where you could work as an assistant to a keeper, or in a safari or wildlife park.
- Make a point of visiting local racecourses and greyhound tracks, paying particular attention to how the animals are treated. Perhaps your local vet has a part-time appointment to treat the horses or dogs. If the offer comes to visit with the vet, you should take it.
- Visit country events such as point-to-point races, even if it is only to see what goes on. One day you may get an admissions interview and the more you know about what happens to animals in different situations, the better.

Case study

James grew up around animals and has always taken a hands-on approach to rearing and looking after them, even getting his own sheep! Although animals have always been a part of his life, he initially started along a different career trajectory before reflecting on his experiences and committing to veterinary medicine.

'I chose to study veterinary medicine so that I could work with animals. I have always had an interest in the care and husbandry of animals, whether that be pets or large farm animals. I was lucky enough to grow up around dogs and cats and large animals such as cows, sheep and ponies. I am really excited to be studying veterinary medicine to continue my journey learning about companion and farm animals and how to treat them. I also enjoy working with people as well, which is important as vets need to be able to communicate well with the animal owners.

'Before applying, I undertook a range of work-experience placements, including one week at a large-animal vets, two weeks at two small-animal clinics, one week at a riding stables, three days with a beef farmer, one day with a shepherd, one week with a farrier and two weeks on a dairy farm.

'Working at small-animal clinics, I was able to follow the day-to-day aspects of the job, such as consultations, vaccinations, spays and neuters. One particular case that fascinated me was a Bichon Frise with chylothorax, where I helped to drain the fluid from the thoracic cavity twice. I saw the dexterity and diagnostic skills required to locate the fluid using an ultrasound scanner and a needle. Seeing emergency cases where the vets did all they could, but ultimately it was kinder to euthanise the animal, highlighted to me the skills required to work in high-pressure situations and to communicate sensitively with emotional owners. While watching a post-mortem on a Rottweiler, I was able to handle some of the tissues and apply my biological knowledge to identify various parts of the anatomy.

'Experience with large-animal vets allowed me to see routine work, such as scanning cows on dairy farms, TB testing and working with farmers to create herd health plans. Helping with TB testing by recording the results of the test and assisting in the successful calving of a Highland cow demonstrated the necessity of good communication skills when working with other vets and the farmers.

'Initially I studied A levels in Maths, Geography and Physics, as well as completing an EPQ and secured good grades (AAB and an A* respectively). I originally pursued mechanical engineering at the University of Nottingham, but not long after I started this degree, I realised that it was veterinary medicine that I really wanted to do. Before making any rash decisions, I undertook work experience with my local farm vets during the Christmas break. This experience made me confident that I would be making the right decision by leaving the engineering course and I went back to college to study A levels in Chemistry and Biology in one year, which was tough but I got A grades and met my offer for vet school.

'I am now in my first year of veterinary medicine at the University of Nottingham. Unfortunately, it has been tainted by Covid-19. The course is fantastic. As overwhelming as veterinary school is at first, I am enjoying the content and the work with animals. Some people find aspects of the course, such as dissection, quite daunting, but it's actually really interesting being able to relate what we have learned in lectures to the cadavers. I prefer working with large animals compared to small animals though!

'In the future, I hope to practise as a farm vet or as a vet in a mixed practice. However, there is still plenty of time left for me to change my mind! My advice for aspiring vets during the application is don't be too hard on yourself, as it is a well-known fact that veterinary medicine is one of the most competitive courses to get on to.'

Variety and staying power

It is crucially important to demonstrate variety in your practical experience with animals. A visit of just one day to a veterinary practice where you watched small-animal work, followed by another visit to a mixed practice where you were able to see a surgical procedure carried out will be impressive, particularly if you can combine this with work at a stables, some contact with local farms, and at least some experience in, for instance, a kennels. The work experience requirements of almost all universities are stringent and require a significant length of time, therefore isolated days are unlikely to carry the same weight, as it should always be about proving your commitment.

But your application to veterinary school will be enhanced even further if, in addition to this, you can demonstrate a convincing commitment to one or two of the local professionals. What will impress people is the fact that you have willingly returned to your local vet's practice over a period of time, and only the vet will know what it has cost you to do this – and the admissions tutors, of course. True, you will have seen a lot of interesting and varied activities and will have met many interesting people, but many of your friends would have melted away had they been asked and expected to do what you have had to do. Let's face it, not many students would have returned to the practice after having to clean up and deal with blood and muck time and again.

If you can demonstrate both a variety of experience and a committed staying power, there is no doubt that this will count strongly in your favour when the competition for places in veterinary school is at its fiercest.

How to get the most out of your work experience

Work experience is more than just a box-ticking exercise to meet the universities' requirements. It is there to confirm your decision to – or dissuade you from – apply(ing) for this course. You might not enjoy your work experience after all; what sounds like a great idea now might be reimagined after a week on a pig farm getting your hands dirty. The key is to go in with an open mind and be prepared for whatever is thrown at you, and never block a request to assist. You are there to help and to learn.

Try things such as:

- keeping a work experience journal (this may be handy in interviews in the future)
- itemising things that you have enjoyed, things that you have found difficult; essentially, what you did, observations you have, things that inspire you and things you might view as negative. What you are looking for is takeaway points that have helped you make this decision to study the course
- talking to as many of the veterinary staff as possible, not only the veterinary surgeons, but also the reception staff and the veterinary nurses; this is a business after all
- talking to pet owners and get to know them and their animals. How easy do you find it to do so? What struggles does this represent for them and for you? How do you find handling the different animals?

Remember that you are lucky to have the opportunity to get this work experience, so approach it with respect. You will find that you might struggle to get some types of work experience because of disease controls and the regulation of contact with infected animals. However, if you cannot get experience in a particular area, do not be dissuaded; rather, keep trying to get similar experience in another place. You may need to readjust your focus to another type of animal, so be flexible.

Work experience during the Covid-19 pandemic

As the Covid-19 pandemic continues to disrupt our daily lives at the time of writing, there is no doubt that it will also impact a student's ability to acquire work experience. While it's not an ideal scenario, veterinary schools have recognised that from March 2020, work experience placements are likely to have been cancelled and, as discussed above, many have lifted specific requirements so that applicants no longer require a specific number of hours or weeks in certain settings. Though admissions tutors can appreciate work-experience placement cancellations, they still expect you to be able to demonstrate a thorough understanding of what the career entails, so you will need to be creative in your approach to gaining this understanding. As well as talking to veterinarians and students, there are online resources, such as virtual work-experience placements, that will assist you in obtaining this knowledge.

Online work experience

As referenced in the specific university requirements section above, many veterinary schools are now considering completion of an online work-experience programme in place of or alongside traditional work-experience placements. The particular course that veterinary schools are recommending is the Virtual Work Experience and Exploring the Veterinary Profession online course, hosted by FutureLearn and developed by the University of Nottingham. All UK vet schools have contributed to its development, and it is viewed as a robust platform that will give you a great insight into the reality of life as a vet. Completing the course will show your motivation and commitment while allowing you to explore veterinary practice in different contexts.

The course can be found at www.futurelearn.com/courses/vet-school-application-support.

Online resources can be especially helpful, but there are other things that you can do to support your application in the midst of a pandemic:

- Keep an eye on the news. Important news relating to veterinary practice can arise, and it is important that you are up to date on topical issues and notifiable diseases.
- Independent learning. Practising veterinary medicine involves a life-long commitment to learning, so taking it upon yourself to learn something animal- or veterinary-related can demonstrate that you are willing to do this. This can involve reading around topics of interest online, such as through the British Veterinary Association's website, listening to podcasts or watching relevant TED Talks. You could also complete an online course, such as those provided by FutureLearn, which usually run over a period of a few weeks.
- Other online resources and social media. Many students and vets present their journeys through social media platforms such as YouTube and Instagram, as well as through blogs. While these are more informal, they can still provide a useful insight into the realities of veterinary medicine as a career.

Fact: Hummingbirds are the only birds who can fly backwards.

4| The 'Jack Russell' Group

Choosing your course

In order to gain a place at university, you must do your research into all aspects of the course. There is no substitute for preparation. There are only a small number of veterinary schools and therefore there is no excuse for a lack of reading into what the courses entail.

Choice of school

Once you have completed your work experience and are certain that you want to be a vet, you need to thoroughly research your choice of veterinary school. When conducting your research, there are various factors you should take into account, including:

- the structure of the course and the teaching styles employed
- the academic requirements needed to gain entry to the course
- the location of the university
- the type of university.

You can obtain this information in a number of ways.

Online information

A straightforward way of accessing information relating to UK veterinary schools is via the UCAS website (www.ucas.com), which often has links to the university websites too. It is important that you commit some time to exploring the information provided on both sites to find the information that you require. This information changes regularly, so if you are researching in advance, check back prior to submitting your application to make sure that nothing has changed. If you are unable to get the answers you need from the internet, do not hesitate to contact the veterinary school directly, either over the phone or via email.

NB: Some veterinary schools offer more than the standard undergraduate veterinary medicine course, including postgraduate degrees, gateway degrees and foundation degrees. Make sure that you are looking at the appropriate course when conducting your research.

Open days

You can learn a great deal about veterinary schools by attending open days. Information about open days can be obtained from university websites, or websites such as www.opendays.com. By attending an organised open day, you will see the specific departments and meet current academic staff and students, who will be able to answer any questions that you might have. You can also get a feel for the university in question – you will be spending the next five years of your life there, so it is important that you feel comfortable in that environment; if you don't, you might struggle to see the course through, irrespective of your academic achievements.

If you are planning on attending an open day, it is important that you book a place on any relevant talks to give yourself the best possible chance of obtaining all the information that you need.

If you are unable to attend an organised open day, you should contact the university and ascertain whether there are any other opportunities to visit the department. In many cases, there will be someone who is able to meet you and give you a brief tour. If this is not possible, you can still visit on an informal basis to have a look around the university and see whether you like it, though you may not be able to visit the vet school itself.

Virtual open days

In light of the Coronavirus pandemic, many universities have converted their open days into virtual events that are conducted wholly online in order to protect the health of prospective students. A virtual open day is different to visiting a campus in person, but it is still an excellent opportunity to see what a university has to offer and get an insight into a place where you might choose to study.

As you won't have to factor in travelling to the universities, you can attend more open days than you might have initially intended. This might open up more doors for you in terms of your veterinary school options.

Virtual open days have differing formats depending on the university, but typically provide an opportunity to look at virtual tours, attend online webinars and talk to current students, lecturers and admissions officers, allowing you to ask any questions that you might have.

League tables

Another useful source of information is university league tables, of which there are many available. However, university league tables do not give a full picture and should be viewed only as one element of the decision-making process. In addition, different league tables use different information to rank vet schools, so it is worth looking into what exactly the positioning is based on. In reality, there is no bad vet school – all are approved by the Royal College of Veterinary Surgeons. It is also worth noting that as there are very few veterinary schools, the league tables will only reveal so much.

One example of a league table is the *Complete University Guide*, which bases its rankings on scores of student satisfaction, research quality and graduate prospects.

Table 2 *Complete University Guide* veterinary school rankings 2021

Veterinary school	Rank
University of Glasgow	1
RVC, University of London	2
University of Bristol	3
University of Edinburgh	4
University of Liverpool	5
University of Nottingham	6
University of Cambridge	7

Source: www.thecompleteuniversityguide.co.uk/league-tables/rankings/veterinary-medicine. Reprinted with kind permission from the *Complete University Guide*.

Course entry requirements

The academic requirements of the ten veterinary schools are similar, but there are some differences and it is important that you obtain the most up-to-date information before deciding where to apply. With regard to the course, be very careful that you are selecting the correct option as there are courses with pre-clinical years and Gateway pathways (see Table 3, pages 52–55) that will not necessarily be what you are wishing to study.

You can get information from:

- university prospectuses
- university websites (more likely to be up to date)
- www.ucas.com
- *HEAP 2022: University Degree Course Offers*, Brian Heap (Trotman Education)
- university admissions staff.

Typical student offers for the academic year 2020–21 are listed in Table 3 on the following pages.

Table 3 Typical student offers 2020–21

University	A levels required	Preferred grades	Access course available	Access course accepted	Subjects required	BTEC accepted	Widening participation policy
Aberystwyth	3	AAA (contextual offer typically ABB when widening participation criteria are met). IB: 7, 6, 6 at Higher level Five GCSEs at grade 7 including biology and chemistry or double award science, with at least a grade 6 in English language, mathematics and physics (if taken as a separate GCSE)	No	Diplomas must be science based and include a minimum of 15 level 3 credits in chemistry at Distinction, as well as a Merit in all other graded level 3 credits Birkbeck College Certificate of Higher Education course in Subjects Allied to Medicine – pass with distinctions in chemistry and biology modules	Biology and chemistry at grade A / Higher level 6	Yes	Yes
Bristol	3	AAA/A*AB (contextual offer typically AAC or A*BC) IB 36 points overall with 18 at Higher level, including 6, 6 at Higher level (contextual offers are 32 points overall with 16 at Higher level, including 6, 5 at Higher level)	Yes (BVSc Gateway to Veterinary Science, D108)	Yes – Access to HE Diploma (Animal Management, Applied Science, Life Science, Medicine or Science) with at least 30 credits at Distinction and 25 at Merit including 15 credits in chemistry and one of biology, physics or mathematics with at least 12 graded level 3 credits in each at Distinction	Chemistry plus one of biology, physics and mathematics (including A level Science practical passes)	Yes – DDD in applied science or animal management, including distinction in science units, and A level Chemistry at grade A	Yes

University	A levels required	Preferred grades	Access course available	Access course accepted	Subjects required	BTEC accepted	Widening participation policy
Cambridge	3	A*AA – subject requirements and specific grade requirements vary depending on college 41-43 overall with 7, 7, 6 – 7, 7, 7 at Higher level. Applicants not classed as mature students (aged 21 or over) are required to sit the Natural Sciences Admissions Assessment (NSAA)	No	An Access to HE Diploma alone is not adequate preparation to study a science subject at Cambridge. Contact the College admissions office to discuss individual circumstances	Chemistry and one or two of biology/human biology, physics or mathematics (Science practical pass) depending on college. See individual college websites for subject requirements	N/A	Yes
Edinburgh	3	AAA (contextual offers are typically AAB) IB 38 points with 6, 6, 6 at Higher level (contextual offers are typically 36 points overall with 6, 6, 6 in Higher level)	No	No	Chemistry and biology and an approved subject (Science practical pass) Good pass in GCSE Physics if not studied at A level	No	Yes
Glasgow	3	AAA IB 38 overall with 6, 6, 6 at Higher level.	No	No	Chemistry and biology with a third science subject recommended	No	Yes
Harper & Keele	3	A level: AAB IB: 6, 6, 6 at Higher level and a minimum of 5, 5, 5 in Standard levels GCSE: Grade 7 in biology and chemistry or science and additional science, and at least a grade 6 in English language, mathematics and physics (if taken as a separate GCSE)	Extended Degree Veterinary Bioscience (with Access to Veterinary Medicine) (XD01) Year 0 and Foundation Programmes at both Harper and Keele	Pass with 45 level 3 credits at Distinction in science based Diplomas, including a minimum of 15 level 3 credits in biology or chemistry and an additional 15 level 3 credits in a second science subject	Grade A in Biology or Chemistry at A level, and a second science subject from biology, chemistry, physics, maths or further maths and statistics 6 in Higher level biology or chemistry and a second science subject	Yes – D*D*D*	Yes

Table 3 Typical student offers 2020–21 (continued)

University	A levels required	Preferred grades	Access course available	Access course accepted	Subjects required	BTEC accepted	Widening participation policy
Liverpool	3	AAA GCSEs: Minimum of seven, with at least three A and four B grades including mathematics, English and physics, either as a standalone or dual award IB 36 overall with 6 in biology and chemistry at Higher Level	No	Yes – Kitemarked level 3 Access to Medicine with a minimum of 15 credits in biology and 15 credits in chemistry Also run a Foundation to Health and Veterinary Studies programme	Biology plus chemistry or another academic science subject (from physics, mathematics, geography, geology or psychology) If chemistry not offered at A level then it must be a minimum of B at AS (Science practical pass)	No	Yes
Nottingham	3	AAB GCSE: Five at grade 7 including biology and chemistry and either physics or maths, with grade 6 in English language and maths IB 34 overall with 6, 6, 5 at Higher level, plus two other supporting level 2 qualifications	D190 course is available with a Gateway year	Birkbeck College Certificate of Higher Education course in Subjects Allied to Medicine – pass with distinctions in chemistry and biology modules	A grades in biology/human biology and chemistry, and B in a third subject (Science practical pass)	N/A	Yes

University	A levels required	Preferred grades	Access course available	Access course accepted	Subjects required	BTEC accepted	Widening participation policy
London (RVC)	3	AAA (contextual offers of ABB for those meeting widening participation criteria) IB: 6, 6, 6 at Higher level with no overall points required GCSE: 7, 7 in biology and chemistry or dual science, with at least a grade 6 in English language and mathematics	Yes – Veterinary Gateway Course (D190)	Diplomas must be Science-based and include a minimum of 15 Level 3 credits in Biology at Distinction and 15 Level 3 credits in Chemistry at Distinction. Merits must be achieved in all other graded Level 3 credits. Birkbeck College Certificate of Higher Education course in Subjects Allied to Medicine – pass with distinctions in chemistry and biology modules	Biology/human biology, chemistry and a third subject (Science practical pass)	Yes	Yes
Surrey	3	AAA/AAB IB 36, with a minimum of 6 at Higher Level including biology and chemistry	No	Yes – including 15 credits (Distinction) each in both biology and chemistry	Biology and chemistry required at grade A Minimum five GCSEs at grade A, including biology, chemistry and physics; English language and mathematics required at grade B (Science practical pass desirable)	N/A	Yes

For A level students, the selectors will take into account:

- GCSE grades (which are just as important as ever without ASs)
- A level choices and predictions or grades
- documentation on any extenuating circumstances that might have affected your performance.

You will be asked for 'good grades at GCSE'. This means lots of grades in the top two bands, particularly in the sciences, English and mathematics. If you did not get good GCSE grades, you can still apply for veterinary medicine, but your referee should make it clear why you did not achieve the grades that you needed – there may have been circumstances, such as illness, that affected your performance. Cambridge Veterinary School states that it has no GCSE requirements as A levels hold greater significance, but it is worth noting that most applicants will hold a strong set of GCSE results.

Every university student has to meet the general matriculation require-ments of each university, but in addition there are the special, prescribed subject requirements. You should check the requirements carefully – the veterinary schools' websites carry the most up-to-date information – but it is likely that you will need three A levels, which will include chemistry, biology and one other science or mathematical subject. Your choice of A level subjects is vital because, although one veterinary school might require two sciences at A level (usually biology and chem-istry), others will require three sciences at A level. If you are applying to Cambridge, you should be aware that different colleges have different requirements.

Currently, no veterinary school makes a conditional offer on three A levels at below AAB grades. Unlike the requirements for many other courses, offers are likely to be made on the basis of A level grades only: stand-alone AS grades are unlikely to be taken into account. However, if you have taken a public exam for your AS at the end of the first year, these grades are important because they will have to be stated on the UCAS application, and thus will give the admissions tutors an indication that you are on course for AAA or higher at A level.

Academic requirements

By the time you read this you will probably have chosen your GCSE subjects or even taken them. If not, here are some points to consider.

- While there are obviously exceptions, most universities specify grades (typically A/7 or B/6) in English language, maths and science subjects (whether dual, triple or core and additional). You will need to carefully research the requirements for each veterinary school and ensure that you meet the requirements before applying.

Many veterinary schools ask for a 'good' set of GCSE results, though what this means exactly can vary considerably.

- Most veterinary schools require A level Chemistry, plus at least one other science or maths. For the most part, the second science subject requested is usually biology. However, there is an increasing amount of flexibility with subject choices.
- Given that the policy for most schools is that AS level examinations are not compulsory, the general stance for veterinary schools is that AS grades will no longer be part of any offers made. If AS level examinations are completed, these are likely to be taken into account by the admissions tutors reviewing your application. If it is your school's policy to sit these exams in year 12, it is important to remember that they are stand-alone qualifications and should therefore be taken seriously.

If you have already taken your GCSEs and achieved disappointing grades, you should carefully research the requirements of each university at GCSE level and identify the universities where you have the best possible chance. If it is genuinely the case, your referee can vouch for you and indicate in your reference that your A level attainment is unlikely to be a reflection of your GCSE performance. To do so, it is crucial that you work extremely hard to prove that this is the case as soon as your A levels begin.

In the case of mitigating circumstances that have impacted your attainment at GCSE, you should contact the university admissions department to ascertain what the required procedure is in that situation. For the most part, a comment from your teacher in your reference will be sufficient, but they may also require a separate form or letter including evidence of the circumstances before they will consider your application.

A level choices

Your choice of A levels

You will see from Table 3 that all veterinary schools now ask for just two science/maths subjects at A level, with the majority still requiring biology and/or chemistry. When choosing your A level subjects, there are three important considerations.

1. Choose subjects that you are good at – you must be capable of achieving an A grade as a minimum requirement. If you aren't sure, ask your teachers.
2. Choose subjects that will help you in your veterinary degree course; life at university is tough enough as it is without having to learn new subjects from scratch.
3. It is wholly acceptable to choose a non-scientific third subject that you enjoy and that will provide you with an interesting topic of

conversation at your interview. With the exception of general studies, critical thinking and, in many cases, further maths, universities do not discriminate based on the third subject. Students who can cope with the differing demands of arts and sciences at A level have an advantage in that they can demonstrate breadth.

Taking four A levels

There's no harm in doing more than three A levels (and an AS exam, if offered by your school), but there is really no advantage to it. In most cases, the added pressure of studying for a fourth A level means that you run the risk of pulling down your overall grade, so you might consider dropping the additional qualification at the end of year 12. Veterinary schools will not include the fourth A level in any conditional offers they make.

The prediction

The admissions tutor will look for a grade prediction in the reference that your teacher writes about you. Your teacher will make a prediction based on the reports of your subject teachers, your GCSE grades and, most importantly, the results of any exams taken at the end of year 12. Consequently, it is vital that you work hard during the first year of A levels in order to get the reference you need.

If there is any reason or excuse to explain why you did badly at GCSE or did not work hard in year 12, you must make sure that the teacher writing your reference knows about it and includes it in the reference. The most common reasons for poor performance are illness and problems at home (e.g. illness of a close relation or family breakdown). In many cases, additional evidence will be required by the university to support this claim, so stating that you underperformed due to ill health when this is not the case is likely to cause bigger problems.

The bottom line is that you need to persuade your school that you are on track for high grades. Convincing everyone else usually involves convincing yourself!

Other qualifications

Scottish Highers

For applicants with **Scottish qualifications**, it is likely that you will be asked for AAAAA–AAABB in your Highers (SCE/SQA) and Advanced Highers in biology and chemistry. Some vet schools like candidates to take a new subject at Higher level if only two Advanced Higher subjects are taken in the sixth year. Highers alone are unlikely to be sufficient.

Irish Leaving Certificate

This qualification is accepted at most universities, and you will generally be expected to get H1, H1, H2, H2, H2, H2 or higher, with H1 in one or both of biology and chemistry. Typically, where physics is not available at leaving certificate level, it will be considered if present at a high grade at junior certificate level.

International Baccalaureate and European Baccalaureate

Another strong sixth-form qualification, the International Baccalaureate (IB) is accepted provided that appropriate combinations of subjects are studied. Three subjects are needed at the Higher level. They typically include chemistry and biology, as well as ideally one or both of physics and mathematics. Grade scores needed at the Higher level are likely to be 7, 7 and 6. If the combination is likely to be different, advice should be sought. Similar subject combinations are required by those offering the **European Baccalaureate**. Applicants are likely to need a score of 80% to 88%, including chemistry and biology.

Extended Project Qualification (EPQ)

The EPQ is there to allow students to independently research and analyse a topic of their choosing. It has been designed to promote a learning style that is independent and thorough, helping students identify with a truly undergraduate way of working. The promotion of these skills and values is held in high regard by a university and often carries more weight than an AS qualification.

In studying an EPQ, students will be able to choose their own topic, be stretched and challenged within that area of research, be largely responsible for their own learning and development and learn new skills, for example, project management and reflection.

The EPQ, for Veterinary Medicine students, can form an interesting basis for discussion at interview. Always remember though, balance an argument if you want to achieve top recognition for it.

The Cambridge Pre-U

The Cambridge Pre-U qualification is becoming more widely understood nowadays as it has been taken up by several leading independent schools. It offers students a different type of qualification for the sixth form, whereby the learning often goes much further, in terms of breadth, and the examining style is more applied, with students requested to apply their knowledge to the questions in a way that most A level syllabuses do not ask of you.

Pre-U grade	A level grade
D1	No equivalent A level grade
D2	A*
D3	A
M1	A/B
M2	B
M3	B/C
P1	C
P2	D
P3	E
U	U

It is important to note that the required qualifications differ between all the universities and therefore you should visit the websites to find the most up-to-date requirements.

Veterinary Gateway pathway

The Veterinary Gateway pathway is a one-year course that is part of an extended six-year veterinary degree programme. It was specifically formulated for those students who are part of the UK Widening Participation cohort – a scheme to get more young people into higher education. It is not applicable to international students. The aim of this course is to enable students who have not met the standard entry requirements to develop their skills over the course of an intensive one-year programme.

There are eligibility criteria that you must meet, which vary between universities but might include criteria such as attending a non-selective state school, having parents that have not attended a higher education institution, and/or having a total household income of £25,000 or less. See www.rvc.ac.uk/undergraduate/vetgateway/index.cfm for more details about the Veterinary Gateway pathway at the RVC

Currently there are gateway courses at Bristol, Harper & Keele, Nottingham and the RVC vet schools.

Checklist

University is about learning, of course, but it is also about the holistic experiences. Remember, university is what you make of it and you have to want to be there after all. It is worth bearing in mind the campus and facilities when making your decision. Think of the distance from home, the distance from the city and the distance from amenities, and make your decision based on these considerations as well. University is as much an experience as it is an academic institution. Try to picture yourself there!

Therefore, consider the following at the application stage.

- Research all of the universities offering the Veterinary Medicine course using their websites.
- Consider the entry requirements as well as the teaching style and the emphasis on practical work and theory.
- Make sure you visit the universities that you wish to apply to and, if you can, attend an open day so that you can meet members of the department and other students to ask any questions you might have.
- While you are limited in the number of veterinary schools that there are, you should still consider whether you want to be on a campus or in a city, as you will be spending a lot of time studying there and you have to make sure it is right for you. Are you concerned by how far you are from home? Is money a worry for you – if so, you might wish to think about living costs in London versus outside of London (see Table 5 on page 156). If you are a sportsperson, have you considered the available facilities on campus? You should have your own personal shopping list and know your requirements; from accommodation to teaching resources, sports teams to leisure facilities.
- Consider the basic and crucial details, such as location, cost, transport, etc. and how these will affect your budget.
- Consider how far you will have to travel, not only home from your lectures but, if you do not drive, what the implications are with public transport for your EMS.
- Consider the size of the university, the number of students on your course, including the ratio of male to female.
- Research what each university is looking for in its candidates to see if you meet its requirements. If you do not, then you probably want to start arranging the work experience necessary and tailoring your application so you are following the exacting standards set down by the university.
- Research the modules available in each course to make sure that the course will offer you what you want to study.

The fifth choice

Although you can apply to a total of five institutions through UCAS, you may apply to only four veterinary schools. What should you do with the final slot? Applying for an alternative, non-veterinary medicine course will not jeopardise your veterinary medicine application in any way, but the fifth choice is still worthy of careful consideration for a number of reasons. There are two main options regarding the fifth choice.

1. Do not include a fifth choice

If you are truly committed to becoming a vet, you need to consider whether you would realistically accept whichever course you include as a fifth choice. If you know that you would not consider that course in place of veterinary medicine and would prefer to reapply, it may be in your best interests to leave the final choice blank. If you were then unfortunate enough to not secure a place to study veterinary medicine, you could spend a year developing your application in order to boost your chances the following academic year.

2. Carefully consider an alternative course

You might choose to include an alternative choice on your form if you are not prepared to wait for a year if your application is unsuccessful, or if you intend to enter veterinary medicine as a graduate.

Trying to combine two different subjects in your personal statement is a recipe for disaster. While admissions tutors cannot see which other courses you have applied for on your UCAS application, the direction of your personal statement will usually signal to both departments that you are not really committed to either course. This would be especially apparent if you were including a subject such as chemical engineering or archaeology as your fifth choice. As such, under no circumstances should this be done; simply stick to veterinary medicine with the personal statement that you use for your UCAS application.

If there is a course that you would genuinely consider studying in place of veterinary medicine, or perhaps you are already reapplying and just want to go to university next academic year, there are ways of applying to two separate courses. For the most part, students will want to apply to another science-based course, which minimises (but does not eradicate) the problems associated with the personal statement.

- If you do intend to include a fifth choice, then you may need to contact the university in question to ascertain whether or not they will consider this application. Many universities will happily consider this option once you have contacted them to explain why your personal statement does not match up with the course, but some may request an additional personal statement. In this case, you must be prepared to deliver a second personal statement outlining why you are committed to studying that course if you are to successfully acquire a place.

- Many students now pursue the option of undertaking a first degree in a related subject, such as bioveterinary science, which they then utilise as a platform to gain access onto veterinary medicine as a second degree.

The pros and cons of undertaking an alternative BSc degree first are considered below:

Cons

- You might spend a whole three years on a course you never really wanted to study. Studying a subject at degree level is an enormous commitment, and if you are not entirely motivated by the content, it can be a very trying time.
- Three years of study will add additional cost and time before actually getting into veterinary school.
- Entry to veterinary school after graduating is not guaranteed.
- If admitted to undergraduate veterinary medicine only, you will still have to study for five more years.
- You might lose focus on veterinary medicine if you study something else first.
- You may not get the student funding and help towards fees for your second degree.

Pros

- Many BSc degrees are in bioveterinary-related subjects – if you don't enjoy this, then are you sure you would enjoy veterinary medicine, which is not that different?
- Veterinary medicine is a lifelong commitment, so two to three years of additional study should not worry you. Becoming a good vet is a journey, not a target.
- Applying as a graduate certainly makes your veterinary school application stronger as you have matured as an individual and academically.
- Having a BSc as well as a veterinary medicine degree may enhance your chances of getting the veterinary job you desire – this is a reason for many students choosing to intercalate.
- Studying a first degree will give you time to mature as a person. You will become acquainted with the demands of university life and develop your skills in independent study. Many students who take this approach find that by the time they reach veterinary school, they are more comfortable with the workload and can approach the study of veterinary medicine with greater confidence.

Fact: A group of owls is called a parliament.

5 | Take the bull by the horns in the cattle market

The UCAS application

Admissions tutors try to get the best students they can for their course, but they are also acting in the best interests of the veterinary profession. They know that the competition is fierce and that the biggest hurdle faced by aspiring students is entry into a veterinary school. Once this obstacle is overcome, there is, given the undoubted ability of those able enough to get the entry grades needed, every chance that with diligence and lots of hard work the student will in due course enter the profession.

However, it is important to understand that motivation is the key factor in selection. It is, in the last analysis, more important even than A levels or their equivalent. Therefore, admissions tutors look at the total impression conveyed by the candidate in their UCAS application. This will include not only academic predictions and their head teacher's report but also extracurricular interests as well as the extremely important supporting practical experience and references. Admissions tutors know that they are exercising a big responsibility: their decisions will largely shape the future profession.

There are various components to a veterinary medicine application that will ultimately determine whether or not you are made an offer. The first component is completion of the UCAS application form. Some sections of the form are purely factual, such as your name, address and prior examination results, as well as a section where you enter your choice of veterinary schools. Perhaps most importantly, you must include a personal statement, which gives you an opportunity to write about why you want to study veterinary medicine and what would make you a good fit for the course and career. In addition, a teacher will provide a reference to support your application.

The application form is critical, as this is what the admissions tutors at each university that you apply to will receive. On reviewing your application, the admissions tutors will make a decision as to whether or not you will be invited to interview. With the exception of one UK veterinary school (University of Bristol), you will need to attend a face-to-face interview in order to gain a conditional offer.

What happens to your application

By the 15 October deadline, vet schools will have received an extremely high number of applications, far exceeding the number of places available. Admissions tutors have the ruthless task of culling applications that are insufficient, and painstakingly reviewing those that remain.

Most vet schools have a well-defined set of criteria that students should consider before submitting an application. Typically, the first part of the selection process by admissions tutors will be ruling out any applicant who does not meet these criteria in full, such as GCSE grades or chosen A level subjects, so it is crucial that you take the time to check that your application won't be thrown out on these grounds. The majority of admissions tutors are happy to discuss these aspects of the application with you, so conduct your research in good time and, where necessary, get in touch with them to see whether you are eligible.

For the most part, students applying to veterinary medicine will have been predicted the required grades (which are typically AAA or higher), or, in some circumstances, may have obtained them already. In addition, a high proportion of applicants will have a good set of GCSE or equivalent results. The academic demands are consistently high with veterinary medicine, so it is unlikely that academic attainment alone will be sufficient to make your application stand out.

This is where the rest of your application comes in, particularly your personal statement and academic reference. The personal statement should discuss your motivation to study veterinary medicine, as well as your work experience and what it has taught you about working in this particular setting. Your reference, usually provided by a teacher at your school, will then discuss your strengths as a student.

In order to decide who to call for interview, the admissions tutors will have to make a decision based solely on the information presented to them. If your application does not demonstrate the necessary requirements at this stage, irrespective of how outstanding your personal qualities are, you will not be invited to interview, which means that the university in question cannot make you an offer. The University of Bristol makes offers for veterinary medicine based on the application process alone, with interviews only taking place in exceptional circumstances.

UCAS Apply

When you apply for UK universities, you do so using the UCAS Apply system. The online UCAS form is accessed through the UCAS website (www.ucas.com). You register online either through your school or college, or as a private individual. Some of the information that you provide on the form is factual, such as where you live, where you have studied, what academic qualifications you have, details of examinations that you are going to take, and which university courses you are applying for. Other sections, such as the personal statement and reference, allow more expansive information to be communicated. The sections of the UCAS form are as follows.

- Personal details: this includes information on you, from your name and address to your fee category status; it also asks you to give someone nominated access to speak on your behalf – make sure this is someone responsible, such as a parent, guardian or adviser.
- Additional information: here you are asked equal opportunities questions, as well as the educational background of your parents.
- Student finance: this section will open if you selected '02 Fee' category in the Personal details section; select your borough so that your local authority will send you the correct information.
- Choices: you have four choices and one non-veterinary science choice to make; most of this section is done through automated lists, though be aware not to accidently select 'live at home' while filling in this section.
- Education: you need to fill in all relevant education for secondary school level, i.e. the establishments where you took examinations. If for any reason you left a school in this time, you still enter it on to the form for transparency. You will also need to include details of your A levels, including any resits.
- Employment: you should only fill in this section if you have done any paid work.
- Statement: this is your opportunity to sell yourself; you have 4,000 characters (including spaces) for the personal statement – write it in Microsoft Word first, although when you copy it across, be mindful of the fact that often the character count may be different because of formatting. Do not worry about spaces in between paragraphs.
- View all details: carefully check through this section and ensure that you have not made any simple errors before submitting the form.
- Reference: once your form is complete, it is sent to the person who will write your reference; they then check it, add the reference and predicted grades and send it to UCAS.
- Pay and send: agree to all the terms and conditions – you will not be able to submit it if you do not – and then pay by credit card.

Despite the help that the electronic version provides, it is still possible to create an unfavourable impression on the admissions tutors through spelling mistakes, grammatical errors and unclear personal statements. In order to ensure that this does not happen, follow these tips.

- Read the instructions for each section of the application carefully before filling it in.

- Double-check all dates (when you joined and left schools, when you sat examinations), examination boards, GCSE grades and personal details (fee codes, residential status codes, disability codes).
- Plan your personal statement as you would an essay. Lay it out in a logical order. Make the sentences short and to the point. Split the section into paragraphs, covering each of the necessary topics (i.e. reasons for wanting to study veterinary medicine, work experience and voluntary work, academic interests and extracurricular activities and achievements). This will enable the selector to read and assess it quickly and easily.
- Ask your teachers to cast a critical eye over your draft, and don't be too proud to make changes in the light of their advice.

Once your application has been submitted, you can keep track of the responses from the universities using UCAS Track.

Applications for veterinary science must be received by UCAS by 15 October for entry in the following year. Applications received after this may be considered by the veterinary schools, but they are not bound to do so, and given the number of applications that they will receive, it is likely that they will not do so. In order to ensure that your application reaches UCAS by the deadline, you should complete it at least two weeks before this date so that your referee has time to write his or her report.

If you are applying to Cambridge, you are required to complete a Supplementary Application Questionnaire (SAQ) by the same deadline of October 15. It is also worth noting that for the majority of UK veterinary schools, additional information is also required through the submission of similar forms and questionnaires. These deadlines vary between universities, but all tend to fall shortly after the official submission deadline for your UCAS application.

Application timeline

The main UCAS submission period is from 8 September to 15 January, but veterinary medicine applications have to be with UCAS by 15 October. Late applications are permitted, although vet schools are not bound to consider them. Ideally, aim to submit your application by mid-September unless there is a good reason for delaying.

Interviews usually take place between November and March of the academic year, so if you have not heard by January, there is still hope.

The timeline below shows the tasks that you will need to be aware of over the course of your A level studies and gives an overview of the timing of some of the various things that you should plan for if you are to maximise your chances of gaining entry into a veterinary school.

Year 12

September: Now is the time to be getting work experience. In reality this should have started earlier than this point; however, there is still time and it should be continuous throughout the year in order to meet the criteria of the individual veterinary schools (see page 39). Work experience is a minimum requirement, so do not forget! The best advice is to get some work experience in every school holiday as well as some part-time weekend work in order to meet the requirements.

May/June: Do some serious thinking about the course you'd like to apply to by conducting extensive research, visiting campuses and discussing your options with admissions tutors and your teachers.

June/July: Make a shortlist of your courses.

August: Finalise your course choices from your original shortlist, making sure that you have met the minimum requirements.

Year 13

September: Complete your application online and submit it to UCAS via a referee. It will be accepted from 8 September onwards.

October: Deadline for applying for places at veterinary school is 15 October. Additional forms and questionnaires need to be submitted by the university-specified deadline.

November: Some universities hold their open days, and interviews can begin from this point onwards.

January: Universities begin to make their decisions if interviews have already been conducted, and offers will be sent directly to you. If you are rejected by all of your choices, you can use UCAS Extra from 25 February to look at other universities.

May: You must tell UCAS which offer you have accepted firmly and which one is your insurance choice by 5 May if you receive all your university decisions by the end of March. If you receive all decisions by 20 May, you must reply to all offers by 10 June. If you receive your final decision by 30 June, your reply date is 13 July.

Spring: Fill out yet more forms – this time for fees and student loans. You can get these forms from your school, college or local authority.

Summer: Sit your exams and wait for your results.

Early July: International Baccalaureate results.

Early August: Scottish Highers results.

Mid-August : A level results. UCAS will get in touch and tell you whether your chosen universities have confirmed your conditional offers.

As you can see, your main task in your first year of sixth form is to start researching your courses and options, organising and carrying out work experience and then preparing your personal statement. The summer between your first and second A level years should be used to continue building your work experience as well as registering and preparing for the Natural Sciences Admission Assessment (NSAA), if you are applying to Cambridge. In the second year, you must hit the ground running, because your UCAS application must be finished by early October and your NSAA will be in early November (check on the Cambridge website for the exam date). At the same time, you must also ensure that you stay on top of your studies so you maximise your chances of achieving the high grades you will need, and you should also start preparing for interview and practising your interview skills. Once your final exams are finished at the end of the year, it is simply a matter of waiting for your results so you can see whether you have secured a place.

Submitting your application

Once you have completed your application and you are totally happy with it you will need to complete the declaration – found under the 'Send to referee' section of Apply. UCAS cannot process your application unless you confirm your agreement with its terms and conditions, which legally binds you to make the required payment. Remember, by clicking the 'I agree' you are saying that the information you have provided is accurate, complete and all your own work and that you agree to abide by the rules of UCAS.

The reference

After you have completed the declaration, your application is ready to be passed to your referee for completion. The reference will be written by a referee who could be your headteacher, housemaster, personal tutor or head of sixth form. They will write about what an outstanding person you are and about your contribution to school life as well as your academic achievement (i.e. on target for at least three A grades at A level), and they will then also give reasons why you are suitable to study veterinary medicine. For them to say this it must of course be true, as referees have to be as honest as possible and they will accurately assess your character and potential to succeed at university. You must have demonstrated to your teachers and other members of staff that you have all the necessary qualities required to become a vet.

Ideally, your efforts to impress them will have begun at the start of the sixth form (or preferably before this); you will have become involved in school activities, while at the same time working hard on your A level subjects and developing strong interpersonal skills, demonstrated by your interactions with staff and students. If you do not feel as though you have done this, don't worry, because it is never too late. Some people mature later than others, so if this does not sound like you, start to make efforts to get involved in the wider life of your school or college, as this will help provide evidence for the people who will contribute to your reference.

References are an important factor since they provide insight into your character and personality. They can also provide significant confirmation of career aims, achievements and interests. The referee's view of your abilities, in terms of analysis, powers of expression and willingness to question things, is the kind of independent information about you that will have an influence with selectors. Additional information about family circumstances and health problems, which candidates rarely offer about themselves, will also be taken into account.

As has already been indicated, performance in A levels (or equivalent exams) is not the sole determinant in selection because of the importance of other motivational factors. However, predicted A level performance is an important aspect for admissions tutors when sifting through and finding committed candidates likely to meet the stipulated academic level. As part of the reference, your referee will need to predict the grades that you are likely to achieve. The most likely minimum requirement for entry is AAA, although some veterinary schools indicate that they may include an A* as part of the offer. If your predicted grades are lower than this, it is unlikely that you will be considered. Talk to your teachers and find out whether you are on target for these grades. If not, you need to do one or all of the following:

- work harder or more effectively, and make sure that your teachers notice that you are doing so
- get some extra help either at school or outside if possible
- communicate with veterinary schools to ask whether they are likely to make you an offer with the grades that you have been predicted
- delay submitting your UCAS application until you have your A level results.

What happens next?

About a week after UCAS receives your application, you will receive an email confirming its receipt. Remember, you will be able to access your application at all times through the UCAS Track system using the same personal ID, username and password that you used to apply.

As soon as UCAS processes your application, your prospective universities can access it, but they will be unable to see the other courses and universities to which you have applied. Once a university has accessed your application, it may contact you to acknowledge receipt of your application; however, not all universities bother doing this, so don't worry if you don't hear from them initially.

From that point on, you should keep a close eye on your emails, as veterinary schools will contact you directly regarding your application. For example, they may send information regarding additional information that needs to be supplied, or to invite you to an interview.

Other supporting documentation

Because work experience in veterinary practices and farms is so important in the selection of applicants for veterinary school, you will be expected to list full details of all such experience. Some veterinary schools will send you a questionnaire asking you to expand on the information you gave about work experience in your UCAS application. Applicants can expect interested veterinary schools to follow up with the veterinary practices and farms where you have worked for additional information about you (this information will be confidential). This is a good sign as it shows that your application has aroused more than a passing interest.

In essence, the veterinary school will ask whether the people you have worked with regard you as a suitable entrant into the veterinary profession. The sorts of issues that concern tutors are:

- general enthusiasm
- ability to express yourself clearly
- helpfulness
- practical ability
- attitude to the animals, to customers and to clerical and nursing staff in the practice – in other words, were you a pleasure to have around?

So, it is clear that the veterinary school can take steps to get hold of additional information about you. You can also help yourself by taking the initiative to gain documentary support. For example, once you have received your UCAS acknowledgement and application number, you can ask the vets with whom you have undertaken your work experience placements to prepare a reference so that once they receive the request from universities, they can send this over promptly. Ideally, this will involve giving details of the work that you did there, with extra details of any interesting cases with which you were involved. This information will go into your file and is bound to help, especially if the vet is able to say that he or she 'would like to see this person in veterinary school'.

Admissions tests

Historically, some veterinary schools required students to sit entrance exams such as the BMAT or UCAT, though these have gradually diminished. For 2020 entry, veterinary school applicants will only need to sit an entrance exam for applications to the University of Cambridge. Cambridge requires vet school applicants to sit the Natural Sciences Admissions Assessment (NSAA), organised by Cambridge Assessment Admissions Testing (www.admissionstesting.org). The exam sets out to assess whether a candidate would be capable of succeeding on an academically demanding degree. It commands an understanding of science and maths, and the specification outlines the specific content that will be assessed in each section (www.undergraduate.study.cam.ac.uk/files/publications/nsaa_specification_2020.pdf). Some questions require application of knowledge, but others command more creative thinking, problem solving and application to unfamiliar context areas. It is therefore designed to determine how you think, rather than what you know.

The NSAA consists of two sections, and each section consists of multiple parts:

Section 1 consists of Part A – Mathematics, Part B – Physics, Part C – Chemistry and Part D – Biology. Students are expected to complete Part A – Mathematics and one other section of their choice within a 60-minute time frame. Each part consists of 20 multiple-choice questions and the use of calculators is not permitted.

Section 2 consists of Part X – Physics, Part Y – Chemistry and Part Z – Biology. Students are expected to complete two sections of their choice within the 60-minute time frame. Each part consists of 20 multiple-choice questions and the use of calculators is not permitted.

The results for each section of the paper are recorded separately. Cambridge do not indicate the scores required as this varies between colleges, but it can be assumed that highly competitive scores are advantageous, as they will indicate who are the most academically able candidates among those with strong academic profiles. As the NSAA can only be taken once a year, there is no opportunity to resit in the same academic cycle.

Preparation for the NSAA should begin in the summer break before you commence your upper sixth studies, in the run up to the exam date in November. In terms of preparation, you should aim to:

- Review the specification for the sections you will study and ensure that you are comfortable with the content being assessed, especially if it is a subject that you are not studying at A level.
- Work through past paper questions in your own time to familiarise yourself with the style of question.

- Work through the past paper questions under timed conditions, as the exam will be time pressured.

UCAS Extra

During the application cycle, if you do not receive any offers in your application, or if you decide that you wish to do something else, you should access UCAS Extra. UCAS Extra gives students a sixth option, though you can only use it if you are prepared to relinquish any offers you hold at the time of accessing it – of course if you have not received any then you will not mind this. It generally operates from late February to early July, during which time universities will advertise courses with spaces through the UCAS website. You can make as many UCAS Extra applications as you wish but not at the same time, only after you have heard from your previous Extra application.

It is rare that UCAS Extra has places for veterinary medicine, but it is worth keeping a close eye on, just in case! It often has related subjects available, however, such as bioveterinary degrees.

What to do if you are rejected

If you are unlucky, you will receive a notification from UCAS telling you that you have been rejected by one or more of the veterinary schools. If this happens, don't despair: you may hear better news from another of the schools that you applied to. If you end up with four rejections, you should take the opportunity to carefully reflect on why your application was unsuccessful. You should contact the admissions departments for clarification, as often they are able to provide some feedback. Remember that veterinary medicine is very competitive, so if you feel that it is still the best option for you, you should take the time to strengthen any aspects of your application that require improvement. Under no circumstances should you give up and decide that it is no longer worth working hard; this will only reduce your chances of making a successful application the following year. Securing the highest possible grades will give you the best chance of submitting a strong application the following year.

If you do secure the grades, it is always worth contacting veterinary schools to ask whether they have spaces available. Due to competition, not all schools will advertise spaces in Clearing, though it is not unheard of for applicants to gain a place this way. If you take this approach because you have secured the necessary grades to study veterinary medicine, then be prepared for an interview at short notice – it is uncommon for veterinary schools to bypass this important step, even through Clearing, as competition will still be high.

In certain cases, if applicants have met or exceeded the grades asked of them by a veterinary school, they are eligible to enter Adjustment through UCAS. However, it's extremely unlikely that the applicant would be able to find another course in veterinary medicine.

Deferring entry and taking a gap year

The UCAS system permits you to apply at the start of Year 13 for entry a year after completion of your A levels. However, you will be expected to meet the conditions of the offer in the year of application. The majority of veterinary schools now welcome students deciding to postpone their entry to the course. The most common reasons given by students are the opportunity to travel, study or work abroad, or to gain additional relevant experience for the course and profession they seek to enter. The latter reason is the one most likely to influence veterinary schools because many applicants do need to strengthen their range of relevant work experience.

It is also an option to wait until you have got your A level grades and then apply in your gap year, as at that point you will have got more work experience, which ultimately is what you need in order to confirm to yourself that this is the right course.

You should be able to explain your plans for the gap year. Do they involve some animal experience? Those coming from urban areas may find that undertaking a gap year of a relevant nature is slightly more difficult to achieve. It is a good idea to discuss this matter on an informal basis with an admissions tutor and get some advice. You will also need to check whether your chosen universities will consider deferred entry or gap year students

Transferring from another degree

If you really want to become a veterinary surgeon, and with hard work you can attain the necessary academic standard, it is not a good idea to take a different degree with the intention of transferring part way through. Some people are badly advised to do another degree and then try to transfer from another course into veterinary science. However, transferring is not feasible because it is necessary to study certain subjects that are exclusive to veterinary science from the beginning: examples are veterinary anatomy and ruminant physiology. In addition, the chance of there being extra places is remote. Transfer then becomes impossible and the only way you could proceed would be to go back and start your veterinary studies at the beginning. Therefore, no one should be advised to take a different course and then try to transfer. Completing an undergraduate degree in a relevant subject and applying as a graduate certainly has its advantages, however – these are discussed in Chapter 4.

Case study

After underperforming in her GCSEs, Georgia started her A levels in non-science subjects as she was told there was no way she could pursue her dream of becoming a vet. After completing her AS exams in these subjects, she changed schools, retook her GCSEs and commenced a new A level programme. Things may not have gone to plan for Georgia, but she has graduated from the world's leading veterinary school, the Royal Veterinary College, with a BSc in Bioveterinary Science and commenced her studies on their veterinary science programme. It's not the route she wanted to take, but when life threw her a series of curveballs, she went along for the ride! Here, Georgia reflects on her journey to vet school and the trials and tribulations that she has encountered along the way. Georgia's story is one of great perseverance and resilience, and shows that with determination and focus, you can always succeed.

'My journey to veterinary medicine has been anything but "easy". As with most veterinary school applicants, I have wanted to become a vet for as long as I can remember. From the moment I began my first work experience placement at the age of 15, I knew this would be my dream job and I would do anything to achieve it.

'The struggles I have faced on this journey, including getting the grades, UCAS applications, interviews and, of course, a global pandemic, have been some of the most difficult challenges of my academic life. If there has been anything that I have learnt from the past six years, it is that perseverance really does pay off and if you want something enough, it will happen!

'I transferred to MPW college from my existing secondary school as not achieving the GCSE grades I had hoped for meant I couldn't study science at A level standard. So, I decided to leave that school, move into the city and get to work. I worked hard for three years, lived away from my family for most of the academic year, and consumed myself in my GCSE and then A level studies. I managed to secure an offer from RVC, my dream university, as well as two others. I was overjoyed! This was going to be my

---

moment. When it finally came to me receiving my A level grades, you can imagine the shock of finding out I had narrowly missed out on the grades I needed for my offer. So ... what now?

'After all of that hard work and accumulating 28 weeks' worth experience to not get a place at vet school, I would be lying if I said I didn't feel like giving up at that moment. My options were to leave everything I had worked towards right there or take up the offer of Bioveterinary Science at RVC, which I could use as a platform to apply for Veterinary Medicine as a graduate. Ultimately, the three-year course at my dream university was a no-brainer and I had to at least try.

'Choosing to move to a solely veterinary-orientated university when you are not studying that degree, and it's your lifelong passion, didn't feel like my smartest choice – it was difficult to be surrounded by what could have been. Studying an academically rigorous undergraduate degree that is not your first choice can be incredibly hard at times, and it can be tough to motivate yourself to keep going.

'There were definitely times when I thought I wouldn't be able to get through it, but immersing myself into university life really helped. I made some really great friends, which made the situation a lot easier. It was great to be able to talk to them (as well as my tutors and my family) about how I was feeling when things were tough – I quickly realised that many people felt the same way as I did and I wasn't on my own. I took part in many social events and joined sports teams and societies. Throwing myself into things taught me to appreciate the experience of university as a whole in my own development.

'My journey to veterinary school may not have been a smooth ride, but looking back on my decisions now, I am really happy with how everything turned out. There are so many benefits of studying for an undergraduate degree before pursuing veterinary medicine that are often overlooked. Some of these benefits are that you are able to get used to the university's way of running things, such as exams, in advance, as well as developing better study habits more aligned with the demands of higher level study. I met some amazing people, including tutors, who led me into avenues of study that I wouldn't have considered otherwise and found that I really enjoyed. In addition, when you come to apply again in the future, you will have an additional three years' worth of experience to talk about, which is always a plus!

'Preparing to apply again for veterinary medicine can be really daunting. You are filled with anxiety about missing out again, and you may worry that you are too old, but in all honesty, none of that matters in the slightest. Make sure you are well prepared and have a good range of work experience to talk about, and the rest will fall into place.

'My top tips for applying to veterinary medicine as a graduate are:

1. Work experience: This can be really difficult to get while studying a full-time degree. You normally have 18 months prior to submitting your application to undertake the required amount of work experience. You really want to avoid doing this in your final degree year as you will have very little time, so I recommend at the end of your second year really cramming in as much as you can, and maybe go lambing for a few weeks over Easter if it's possible around exams.

2. Hobbies: One thing I learnt from my endless experience with veterinary medicine applications is that they really want to know who you are and what you enjoy outside of the scientific community. It's great that you wrote a 35-page research article on the effects of Bovine Viral Diarrhoea Virus on the expression of genes associated with pregnancy recognition in cattle, but they want to see who YOU are! Take up painting, go rock climbing – the world is your oyster!

3. University life: This point is an extension from the last, try and get involved in university clubs and social events as much as possible. Get to know the lecturers and become an active member of the university. It helps to show on your application that you have really taken advantage of being an undergraduate student and why they should want you to contribute to their university!'

'My one final piece of advice for any Bioveterinary Science undergraduate that wants to become a vet is that this degree is just a stepping stone to get you to where you want to be. It's not forever, and it doesn't mean you will be any less of an amazing vet! If anything, it will make you a lot more competent than most of the first-time degree vets, believe me! Applying to postgraduate veterinary medicine li another challenge in itself, but it's not impossible. The only thing you need is belief in yourself and a lot of determination. Work hard and you will reap the benefits!'

Fact: Young goats pick up accents from one another.

6 | No one likes a copycat
The personal statement

One of the most important parts of your application is your personal statement, as this is your chance to show the university selectors three very important themes:

1. why you want to be a vet
2. what you have done to investigate the profession
3. whether you are the right sort of person for their veterinary school (in other words, the personal qualities that make you an outstanding candidate).

A typical personal statement takes time and effort to get right; don't expect perfection after one draft.

When it comes to distinguishing between highly qualified candidates, one of the most important factors that is considered is the personal statement. If this is badly worded, littered with errors or lacking detail about the attributes and experiences of the candidate, it may well be rejected out of hand. Ultimately, the more thought that you give to your UCAS application and personal statement, the better they will be and the greater your chance of being asked to attend an interview and made a conditional offer.

Another important consideration is that your personal statement must be no more than 47 lines long or 4,000 characters (including spaces); this is a strict limit and so you need to ensure that you are as close to this as possible.

Sections of the personal statement

Why veterinary medicine?

Your personal statement must, fundamentally, convince admissions tutors of your interest in following a career in veterinary medicine.

A high proportion of UCAS applications contain a sentence like, 'From an early age I have wanted to be a vet because it is the only career that combines my love of science with the chance to work with animals.' Admissions tutors get bored with reading this, and it doesn't necessarily highlight your desire to study veterinary medicine: there are many careers that combine science and animals – it is not exclusive to being a vet.

However, the basic ideas behind this sentence may well apply to you. If so, you need to personalise it. You could mention an incident that first got you interested in veterinary medicine – a visit to your own vets for work experience or with your pet, a conversation with a family friend, or a lecture at school, for instance. You could write about your interest in biology or a biology project that you undertook when you were younger to illustrate your interest in science, and you could give examples of how you like to work with animals. The important thing is to back up your initial interest with your efforts to investigate the career.

It is a common misconception that you need to begin your personal statement with an inspirational quotation or grand statement; again, admissions tutors get bored of students trying to squeeze in lines from books, poems or films that have no real meaning to the applicant. What an admissions tutor would rather see is a statement of the genuine reasons that you want to study veterinary medicine, written in clear, uncomplicated English.

Another common pitfall of the first paragraph is taking up valuable space with an explanation about what the subject is about or what the profession entails. Remember that the people reading your statement know exactly what the profession is about and so do not need to be lectured on it! Instead, you need to take the time to explain about your *own* interest in the profession and why you feel compelled to follow this career path.

Finally, don't be afraid to lean on your work experience placements or voluntary work here. Often, those initial sparks of interest in a career in veterinary medicine are underpinned by what you observed when shadowing a vet in practice or on a farm. This section of the personal statement should be sizeable, so it is a good idea to link your motivation to study veterinary medicine in with your experiences. These experiences will also form a significant proportion of your personal statement.

Work experience and voluntary work

This section is important to demonstrate that you gained something from your work experience placements, and that they have given you an insight into the profession. When discussing your veterinary-specific experiences, you should give an indication of the length of time you spent at each placement and the impressions you gained. You could comment on what aspects of veterinary medicine attract you, or on what you found interesting or on something that you hadn't expected, but remember that this is not a shopping list. You are not simply reeling off experience after experience; you are expected to provide deeper reflection about what you have seen. Beyond this, you should also mention any other work experience or voluntary work you have had in a relevant role and what you learned from it. Although you may not think of these sorts of experiences as being relevant, they can often demonstrate to an admissions tutor good interpersonal skills or commitment and dedication, all of which are relevant to veterinary medicine.

It will be far easier to write this section of your personal statement if you kept notes in a reflective journal during your work experience. Look back over what you wrote and use your thoughts and experiences as a stimulus for this section. With luck, the admissions tutors may pick up on these experiences at interview and ask you to expand on some of your comments.

Following this, you should discuss the experiences you have had while undertaking any voluntary work. Any type of voluntary placement is a useful addition to your statement, but ongoing work in an animal-based setting really boosts your profile. Opportunities often exist in animal charities, and it is worth trying to contribute regularly over a long period of time rather than carrying it out for just a week or two. This type of experience can help you get an insight into animal handling and care. As with any animal-based work experience, you should make a note of any key experiences that you have and what they have taught you, as this can then be commented on in your personal statement.

Given the Covid-19 pandemic, there is an understanding from veterinary schools that you may not have been able to carry out work experience or voluntary work as planned. The important thing to remember is that admissions tutors are looking for a thorough understanding of the veterinary profession and what the role of a vet entails. This can be achieved through talking to veterinary students, veterinary surgeons and other professionals in animal-based roles, online research (including social media, blogs and vlogs), online learning (such as free courses), keeping an eye on the news, and even virtual work experience opportunities.

Your academic interests

It is important for your personal statement to contain information about your academic interests and how they have furthered your desire to study veterinary medicine. This may be related to some topics or practical skills that have been of particular interest to you over the course of your A level studies, or to an interesting article you have read in a newspaper or journal, or to something engaging you heard in a lecture. Whatever it is, it will help to demonstrate your desire to pursue the course, as long as you make it relevant to veterinary medicine and put in sufficient detail. In so many personal statements, this section struggles to get beyond, 'I enjoyed learning about animal physiology' and 'I enjoy using different apparatus in practical work'; however, this is too generic to be meaningful. Keeping a journal over a long period of time of any wider reading that is relevant to veterinary medicine will help this section to genuinely reflect what your interests are rather than being based on what you have panic read the week before submitting your application.

Evidence of developing skills and personal qualities

The person reading your UCAS application has to decide two things: whether you have the right skills and personal qualities to become a successful vet, and whether you will be able to cope with and contribute to veterinary school life. To be a successful vet, you need (among other things!) to:

- successfully pass your undergraduate studies
- have good interpersonal skills and get on with a wide range of people
- be able to work under pressure and cope with stress
- have well-developed manual skills.

How, then, does the person reading your personal statement know whether you have the qualities they are looking for? What you must remember is that the admissions tutor doesn't know you, so you have to give lots of evidence of how you have demonstrated and developed these qualities. Some of the things they may be looking for are:

- skill development during work experience/voluntary work
- positions of responsibility
- work in animal-based environments
- an ability to get on with people
- participation in activities involving manual dexterity
- participation in team events
- involvement in school plays or concerts.

Some examples of aspects that you might want to include in your application are detailed below.

Have you demonstrated a range of interests?

Veterinary schools like to see applicants who have done more with their life than work for their A levels and watch TV. While the teacher writing your reference will probably refer to your outstanding academic achievements, you also need to say something about your achievements in your personal statement. Admissions tutors like to read about achievements in sport and other outdoor activities, such as the Duke of Edinburgh's Award Scheme. Equally useful activities include Young Enterprise, charity work, public speaking, part-time jobs, art, music and drama.

Bear in mind that admissions tutors will be asking themselves: 'Would this person be an asset to the veterinary school?' Put in enough detail and try to make it interesting to read. An important point to note though is that extracurricular information must not take up more than about 25% of your personal statement, as the primary focus is on why you want to get in to veterinary medicine.

The key is to ensure that you are always relating your personal qualities and extracurricular activities to your application, in order to show evidence of the attributes and skills needed to become a vet.

Have you contributed to school activities?

This is largely covered by the section on interests, but it is worth noting that the selector is looking for someone who will contribute to the communal life of the veterinary school. If you have been involved in organising things in your school, do remember to include the details. Don't forget to say that you ran the school's fundraising barbecue or that you organised guest speakers for the Biology Society. Conversely, veterinary schools are less interested in applicants whose activities are exclusively solitary or cannot take place in the veterinary school environment.

The admissions tutors will be aware that some schools offer more to their students in the way of activities and responsibilities than others. However, even if there are very few opportunities made available to you through your school, you must still find ways to gain experience and develop your skills. You don't have to have been captain of the rugby team or gone on a three-month expedition to Borneo to be considered, but you do need to be able to demonstrate that you have made efforts to participate in a range of worthwhile activities.

Have you any achievements or leadership experience to your credit?

Admissions tutors are particularly attracted by excellence in any sphere. Have you competed in any activity at a high level or received a prize or other recognition for your achievements? Have you organised and led any events or team games? Were you elected as class representative to the school council? If so, make sure that you include this in your personal statement.

Summary

If you are really struggling with what to include in your personal statement based on the sections outlined above, answering the questions below will provide a good starting point.

- Why do you want to be a veterinary surgeon? There are many possible reasons and this is where your individuality will show.

- Outline your practical experience. Give prominence to the diverse nature of it, the clinics, farms, stables, etc. you have worked at or visited.
- Mention any specific interesting cases that you witnessed or assisted with and, importantly, what you learned from them.
- You like animals, but how do you respond to people?
- How did you get on with vets, nurses and the customers? Any teamwork experience?
- Give an indication of your career direction, even if it is tentative at this stage. Show that you have thought about the possibilities.
- Have you had any special achievements or responsibilities connected either with animals or with an outside interest?
- List other activities and interests of a social, cultural or sporting kind. Here is your chance to reveal more about yourself as an individual.

Things to avoid

Writing your personal statement can be a difficult and long-winded process. There are some easy things to avoid that will ensure that you make a good impression with your application.

Not enough words

While most people will have the opposite problem of having a personal statement that is too long, you must ensure that it is as close to the 4,000 character limit as possible. Anything significantly below the character count will make a negative impression on the admissions tutors.

A lack of detail or reflection

It is crucial that you do not simply list your experiences, but carefully reflect on them to ensure that the admissions tutors can see that you have gained a lot from them. When discussing work experience, go into detail about what you witnessed and reflect on what you learned. When giving details of what you are studying, be specific about topics you have enjoyed. This will give the admissions tutor a much greater insight into who you are and the skills you possess.

Not being very personal

Make sure your personal statement has evidence and experiences to show an admissions tutor who you really are and what you are genuinely interested in.

Negativity

Unfortunately, many personal statements contain negative points about things that an applicant hasn't enjoyed studying or things they might not like about the career. These are sometimes included due to a misguided need to be brutally honest, or to show that you thoroughly understand all aspects of the profession, but this really is not necessary. The overall tone should be optimistic and positive throughout.

Lecturing about veterinary medicine

Statements can often waste time by listing facts about veterinary medicine or what vets do. Remember that the people reading your statement will know all of this.

Discussing money and potential earnings

Although most veterinary medicine applicants will have thought about how much money they will be making at some point, it is not something that needs to be highlighted in your personal statement. Your reasons for studying veterinary medicine need to run much deeper than this if you are going to get into veterinary school.

The use of overused, repeated stock phrases

Commonly used statements can make an admissions tutor question whether your statement is an accurate picture of who you are. If you genuinely want to express a generic idea, think of how you could expand on it in your own words to make it more meaningful.

Losing the focus on veterinary medicine

If your personal statement only really comes alive is when you are discussing how much you enjoy studying English Literature, then you are misusing the space that you have available. Transfer that enthusiasm to elements of your personal statement that the admissions tutors will want to see.

Overusing the thesaurus

Beware of overusing a thesaurus. Obviously, you want your English to be as good as possible, but make sure that what you have written makes sense and sounds like you.

Example Personal Statements

The example personal statements below show how an applicant might structure their personal statement.

It is impossible to pick one of these personal statements as the definitive article because they are all individual. There are no right or wrong answers, only a correct template or model to use. As long as the personal statement *is* personal and means something to you, you will have achieved your goal.

Remember: be concise and try to be unique. This does not mean be extrovert, it just means make it honest to you. How? Relate it back to you and what skills and abilities you can bring to the role and what have you done to hone these skills over time – it may be in different activities and that in itself is original. You are never going to be the same as someone else, though you will have similar work experience because you are following a guideline. Therefore, establish what it is that makes you different and what you really want the university to know about you. Then sell it.

Example personal statement 1 (3,990 characters with spaces)

Our home was like a small rehab centre. Even before knowing that veterinary practice was a profession, I was helping my parents treat sick and injured stray animals. Back then I thought this was the norm never realising that my passion would lead me to something beneficial in the future. My dedication to animals has brought me this far.

When I was old enough to know I wanted to be a vet I started placements, internships and courses, all of which have confirmed my commitment to the profession. Living in geographically and culturally diverse places, such as Turkey, China, South Africa and Sweden, I have come to appreciate the commonalities, regulatory requirements and technical practices and the differences in the profession. My blog www.born-to-be-a-vet.com describes my experiences at vets' surgeries, a university anatomy class, a university farm, a ranch, a cattery, a wildlife reserve and voluntary work.

Volunteering for six months at an international pet hospital and clinics in Turkey, UK and China enabled me to become involved in consultations, clinical case discussions and various surgeries, including castrations, ovariohysterectomies, toe amputation and mass removals, providing invaluable experience. Observing vets analyse test results and write prescriptions taught me the importance of chemistry in veterinary studies. Dealing with emergencies and routine management at a cattery taught me to respond sensitively to delicate situations and empathise with owners prompting my choice of A level Psychology. I am aware of the application of the study of psychology in animal care and welfare, and am acquiring skills and an understanding that will enhance my ability to deliver veterinary medicine.

Working with wild animals at an African game reserve gave me a completely different insight. I experienced a mix of emotions from the satisfaction of helping a hyena return to life to the sorrow of putting young, healthy puppies to sleep, due to financial constraints on the owners, and even using one of them as a cadaver for autopsy. There I witnessed the impact of finances on shelter vets' conditions as opposed to private vets.

Taking the Vetsim and VetMedic courses at Nottingham University I became enthralled not only by the practical and technical elements of being a vet, but also by research, conferences and investigative work, including a genetic engineering session with an opportunity to create my own laboratory species.

During my internship at the research farm of Ankara University, I handled cattle and sheep daily. I also had the chance to be a guest student at the Veterinary Faculty, joining the laboratory sessions and working on cadavers' digestive and respiratory systems, thus realising the importance of studying biology at A level.

I have organised and volunteered in community projects, such as saving new-born sea turtles which showed me how important even one life is for ecology. I am a show jumper and have been riding since I was four. Owning horses and shadowing stable vets for several years taught me how to treat basic illnesses, what to do in emergencies and the importance of prevention techniques. I have several medals for a range of sports, including second place in show jumping at the Longines China Tour. I was also commended by the Chamber of Commerce. Sports and arts have helped in shaping my personality.

As a well-travelled, trilingual young adult, I have had the privilege of living and studying overseas among many cultures which has taught me global tolerance, acceptance and empathy. I am a very sociable and conscientious person with a strong work ethic and an absolute determination to aim high. My ability to work both on my own and in teams as well as in stressful conditions has helped me to pursue my goal of becoming a vet. I cannot wait to conduct research and academic work and participate in clinical and public-health work. For me this is a real opportunity to help animals, their owners and everyone in that community.

Notes on personal statement

- Makes interesting comparisons between working in clinics in different countries.
- Has a variety of work experience.
- Considers A levels here.
- Gives a little context about herself.
- A bit too general in places with her work experience.
- A little too idealistic in places.

Example personal statement 2 (3,983 characters with spaces)

Watching my first dog spay at the age of 14, I was fascinated by the absolute precision of the veterinary surgeon as they skilfully manoeuvred the tissues and delicate vasculature. After this, I knew with absolute certainty that the veterinary profession was for me. My desire to strengthen my veterinary knowledge has grown exponentially and I have fully immersed myself in all aspects of the profession.

After engaging in 18+ weeks of veterinary work experience, both locally and internationally, I have a comprehensive understanding of the challenges faced by veterinarians on a daily basis in a wide range of environments. Spending four weeks in various small animal clinics allowed me to observe the intricacies of small animal practice and the importance of inter-personal skills when dealing with clients; for example the delicacy and empathy required in a terminal canine carcinoma case.

During a six-week, self-funded placement in a mixed clinic in Ghana I was able to see the opposite end of the scale where financial concerns frequently supersede animal welfare and where the attitude to veterinary care is vastly different. During this placement I was responsible for preliminary checks during consultations, drawing up and helping to administer medication and assisting in surgeries. I was fortunate enough to help close after a hernia repair in a sheep by performing several simple interrupted stitches. Assisting in an ear-cropping surgery reinforced the ethical concerns associated with this practice. The need for problem-solving skills was imperative for making the most of limited resources, for example when making a make-shift cast out of masking tape and a swab sample tube for a two-week-old kitten with a suspected fractured leg.

During several weeks spent lambing and on a dairy and poultry farm, I learnt to appreciate how vets contribute to human health by ensuring the quality of our meat and milk while balancing the needs of the farmer with concerns for the animal's quality of life. A day at an abattoir fortified this. I thoroughly enjoyed the hands-on nature of lambing, and I admired the fast-thinking of the farmers in critical situations. During a week on the road with a farm vet, I observed an emergency bovine caesarean, assisted in a difficult pygmy goat birthing and helped with de-horning 60 calves.

A week with an equine vet and another at a specialist equine hospital taught me about the intricacies of metabolic disorders and diagnostic options when dealing with lameness. I was also able to observe a suspensory ligament neurectomy. A week at a stud farm enhanced my understanding of the care of elite sports horses and introduced me to the complexities of breeding. Having owned my own horses I am very comfortable in an equine environment, and competing at national level has taught me discipline, dedication and teamwork. I worked as a riding instructor at a riding stables for several years which developed my leadership and communication skills.

Additionally, during a week at a zoo I learnt about the importance of nutrition and intellectual engagement of wild species.

While participating in my Duke of Edinburgh Gold Award and during regular meetings as a charity rep at school, I developed a passion for volunteering and charity work. I volunteered at a school in Kenya where I was responsible for a class of 20 pupils for six weeks. On my return I have raised £2,000 and have independently set up a 12-month renovation project, which has reinforced the importance of organisation and perseverance.

At university, I have volunteered and fundraised for Guide Dogs and attained my Level 1 My Guide certificate. I am also a STEM Ambassador, whereby I travel to disadvantaged schools to engage children in scientific activities and help them broaden their horizons. This will be a valuable experience for explaining diagnoses to families as I'm well practised in explaining scientific terms in a way children can understand. I am also an active member of the biology, snowsports and art societies, and this year I hope to participate in CommuniTea, a student-led association that organises tea parties for elderly people in care homes, as well as becoming a zoology specimens volunteer.

Key modules in my biology degree, such as parasitology and immunology have allowed me to draw interesting parallels across human and veterinary medicine, while statistical and bioinformatics modules have advanced my mathematical and analytical problem-solving skills.

I am enthusiastic, self-motivated and dedicated to the veterinary profession. I believe my strong problem-solving skills and intellectual curiosity make me very suitable to this dynamic career and I look forward to performing my first dog spay.

Notes on personal statement

- A very good level of relevant work experience.
- Includes a variety of experiences and, importantly, what was learnt from them.
- Shows commitment.
- Shows an understanding – and value – of research.
- A little too narrative in places.
- Starts to read a little like a shopping list when the zoo is mentioned, and that paragraph could have been further developed to illustrate the difference between the types of animals cared for in a zoo versus those in a small veterinary practice.

Example personal statement 3 (3,995 characters with spaces)

Standing knee-deep in mud, desperately trying to prevent an embryo from defrosting as the local vet manoeuvred a heifer into the crush, is perhaps my most vivid memory of my placement in Ireland. However it was in that crucial moment, despite the torrential rain and the angry cows, that I realised that the prospect of a career in veterinary medicine provided enough drive to overcome the significant hurdles that pursuing it would present.

In pursuit of a career in this field, I have explored all aspects of veterinary medicine, from the highs of bringing new life into the world during lambing season to the lows of euthanasia within a small practice. From working on a 22,000 sow unit to implanting over 100 CIDRS on a cattle farm, I am constantly left in awe at the intricate complexity of animal biology. These placements have demonstrated a wide array of possibilities in terms of an ultimate career choice, and the refined skill set I will need to develop to excel within them. My weekly placement at my local practice has allowed me to develop practical skills such as bandaging, intubation and suturing, as well as allowing me to effectively deal with patients as well as owners in sensitive situations. The future of veterinary medicine excites me; the possibilities of biomechanics and new developments in oncology that I witnessed while attending specialist lectures at congress were particularly fascinating. Most recently, I volunteered at a wildlife sanctuary in Australia which allowed me to work alongside native fauna and research one of Australia's most prevalent animal diseases, Koala Retrovirus. This enabled me to consider developing treatment concepts against the slow metabolic rate and increased antibiotic half-life of koalas, such as nano-medicine, and how this could allow for an effective way of treating koalas suffering from a compromised immune system to be discovered.

By studying biology, I have been able to develop a strong understanding of physiology, from the basis of movement through antagonistic muscle action to resistance against infection by the immune system. In practice, I have witnessed the importance of having a strong scientific knowledge in order to recognise symptoms and act accordingly in terms of diagnostics and treatment. Studying chemistry has enlightened me to the intricate nature of pharmacology, and how the precise structural formula of a drug is so important to the outcome of the patient. The significant development of my problem-solving skills through the study of chemistry will also prove to be undoubtedly useful when facing the diagnostic puzzles of veterinary medicine. My analytical skills have developed significantly through the study of English literature, which became useful upon helping a vet diagnose a complex case of canine pyometra in which I was able to interpret ultrasound scans and contribute towards the final diagnosis. My EPQ on neurodegenerative diseases in ruminants allowed me to study a complex organ in detail and further increased my fascination of livestock diseases. Over the year, I also plan to take an Artificial Insemination course to further improve my livestock handling skills.

I have been running a blog on my university application since 2015, accredited by organisations such as *Veterinary Times*. My articles have been featured both online and in my college's magazine. I am also an author and editor for the *Young Scientist*

Journal where I had an article published on the use of Tyrosine Kinase Inhibitors in veterinary chemotherapy. Attending events such as VetFest and VetsSouth have expanded my knowledge and allowed me to converse with some of the world's most talented veterinarians. My unyielding passion for the field, combined with my philanthropic nature, enthusiasm for scientific research and work experience to date, have consolidated my belief that studying veterinary medicine is the perfect career choice for me.

Notes on personal statement

- This is clearly based on real experience and shows an understanding of the realities of veterinary medicine as a career.
- Reflects carefully on academic background, including supercurricular activities conducted, such as the EPQ and article and blog writing, which highlight a genuine interest in the subject.
- There isn't enough space available to discuss all possible work experience placements in depth, highlighting the importance of selecting those that best demonstrate your understanding of the field.

Example personal statement 4 (3,980 characters with spaces)

My ambition to become a large-animal vet stems from not only a fascination of the sciences but also the ability to work with and help animals and people simultaneously. My work experience demonstrated to me the impact vets can have for both large- and small-animal owners, some of whose livelihoods depend on the welfare of their animals.

Completing the online course 'Do you have what it takes to be a veterinarian?' reinforced my passion and gave me an insight into the complexities of becoming a vet. Working at small-animal clinics, I was able to follow the day-to-day aspects of the job, such as vaccinations, spays and neuters. One particular case that fascinated me was a Bichon Frise with chylothorax. I helped the vet drain fluid with a syringe from the thoracic cavity twice. I saw the dexterity and diagnostic skills required to locate the fluid using an ultrasound scanner and a needle. Emergency cases where the vets did all they could but ultimately decided it was kinder to euthanise the animal, highlighted to me the skills required to work in high-pressure situations and to communicate sensitively with emotional owners. While watching a post-mortem on a Rottweiler, I was able to handle some of the tissues and apply my biological knowledge to identify the various parts of anatomy.

Experience with large-animal vets allowed me to see other routine work, such as scanning cows on dairy farms, TB testing and working with farmers to create herd health plans. Helping the vet to record the results of the TB tests and assisting in the successful calving of a Highland cow, showed me the necessity of good communication skills required to work with the other vets and the owners of the animals. Working on a dairy farm demonstrated to me the reality of working with large animals. I witnessed stillborn calves and diseases such as foot rot; dealing with these problems while still running a profitable business can be demanding.

Being responsible for mucking out, feeding the calves and helping to milk, I learnt the impact that good quality bedding has on illness, the importance of good hygiene in the parlour as well as how to check for mastitis. I developed my sheep-handling skills while helping a shepherd vaccinate, fly treat and worm lambs. I realised the importance of good-quality animal-handling systems and that organisation is key for minimal stress when working with a flock or herd. I reinforced this skill while I worked with a beef farmer to move cattle and tag fresh calves. Working at a livery yard and shadowing a farrier showed me the importance of good limb conformation and foot balance; this prevents concussive injuries within the foot, such as splits or cracks, and also helps the rest of the musculoskeletal system.

Studying A level Biology and Chemistry has allowed me to gain a better understanding of particular diseases such as Bovine Spongiform Encephalopathy (BSE) and apply my knowledge of protein structures and protein folding to understand more about the causive agent, the Prion. I have learned about the importance of disease surveillance in food-producing animals and how diseases such as BSE and TB have such a large impact on animal and human health combined.

Having competed internationally for GBR in sailing competitions in a two-person skiff, I am well equipped to deal with high-pressure situations and quick decision making, both individually and as a team. This is also demonstrated by my Bronze and Silver DofE awards and being part of school CCF. I am a confident communicator, who is able to participate and contribute in discussions and meetings. Being a UK 29er Class committee member reinforced my communication and organisational skills. I enjoy wildlife photography, clay pigeon shooting, going out with my local Young Farmers group and looking after my Ryland ewe lambs. A veterinary degree would allow me to pursue my fascination of large-animal health management, ruminant digestion and become a large-animal vet.

Notes on personal statement

- Shows an understanding of the role of vets, especially when dealing with owners.
- Shows commitment by undertaking an online course.
- Consistently links work experience observations back to their significance, rather than listing.
- While the focus of the personal statement should be on enthusiasm for veterinary medicine, very little else is covered that gives an insight into this person and their academic knowledge.

Example personal statement 5 (3,989 characters with spaces)

Veterinary medicine to me is doing everything within your power to make an animal's life better, regardless of circumstance. Between the ages of 14 and 17, I volunteered at a local animal rescue centre, helping the abandoned animals and examining them for injury, as well as dealing with customers to ensure that each pet adopted would be well looked after. This revealed to me how many pets are mistreated because owners get bored of them, making me determined to pursue a career in veterinary medicine and to help prevent these types of avoidable suffering.

Work experience at a referral veterinary practice enabled me to compare how different specialist cases are treated compared to those at a primary vet practice. During my time there, I watched two phacoemulsifications, as well as an endoscopy, colonoscopy and other specialist operations. I learned that vets must be quick thinking and have a broad knowledge to present a diagnosis within the short consultation period. From watching the surgeons, I discovered the importance of determination and resilience to ensure the patient has the best possible chance of a good outcome. While working on farms I learned the importance of colostrum for calves and how farmers must ensure that each calf receives the correct start to protect them from infection for the rest of their lives. This taught the importance of being attentive when working with any animal, ensuring that a problem is quickly detected so that a solution can be made before the danger increases. I also saw how farm work is more business orientated; that both profits and animal welfare must be considered.

Training Guide Dog puppies for the past seven years has shown me just how important animals can be to a person's life, and how to maintain a fast-track training schedule for young puppies, while allowing them to grow and have fun to create healthy assistant dogs. I have also attended Vetquest at the University of Bristol, giving me an insight into life as a vet as well as student life.

Through A level Biology I have developed a strong interest in antibiotic resistance and its effects on both animals and humans. My research into ways to reduce resistance, such as how to penetrate the structure of gram-negative bacteria, has opened my mind to the variety of possible solutions still to be discovered. Leading the school dissection club enabled me to visualise the organs and to put my anatomy knowledge into context. I taught the structure and functions of a pig's pluck to younger students – examining each component individually and as a complex of organs – and pigs' trotters, investigating their advantageous characteristics. This gave me leadership skills and confidence when working in a group. In chemistry, I have always been intrigued by how small molecular variation causes dramatic effects, shown by the effect of thalidomide causing limb defects. This increased my understanding of the minute details that can have large impacts on reaction products, and through this I developed an interest in the role of drug testing to ensure that negative side effects are kept to a minimum.

Last summer I went to Borneo, spending time in both the primary and secondary jungle showed me the massive impact palm oil extraction is causing to the habitats there, even after being regrown. During time at Danum Valley conservation centre, I went on hikes through various areas of the jungle, and glimpsed some of the species living there, such as orangutans, monkeys and many insects. As a primary jungle under conservation I was able to see how jungle life thrives without the destruction caused by humans.

A course in photography enabled me to see the world from a new angle and I learned about the range of manual settings to use depending on the style of photo you are after. I play the viola in an orchestra and to grade 7, which has highlighted to me the importance of understanding each feature of your team to work together in harmony.

Notes on personal statement

- Interesting contextualisation.
- Range of work experience.
- Good links between study and veterinary medicine.

Example personal statement 6 (3,991 characters with spaces)

I grew up surrounded by ducks and chickens, and breeding poultry for three years with the use of an incubator gave me an early introduction to veterinary science. This experience allowed me to follow the life cycle of these birds, tracking their embryonic physiology and growth through the use of candling the eggs, which fascinated me. My choice of A level subjects helped develop my analytical skills, allowing me to engage in debates and strengthen my reasoning ability. Studying biology gave me an insight into the anatomy and pathogens of animals, as well as the biotechnological processes required to manufacture medicines and genetically manipulate genes and cells for transplant. Chemistry has made me more aware of the fundamental molecules that make up organisms and our environment.

My work experience has further motivated me, and my three weeks' experience at a small-animal practice enabled me to shadow a vet's daily routines as well as observing the work involved both in the operating theatre and in dealing directly with animals and their owners. This gave me an insight into the qualities required by a veterinary surgeon, who must show patience and precision in surgery, as well as compassion and communication skills during consults. My week at Seers Croft Practice was of particular interest as working in their specialist unit enabled me to see reptiles being treated. A particular highlight was monitoring a tortoise recovering from a spay operation; the care and expertise involved in dealing with such a specialised animal was instructive and rewarding.

A week on a farm allowed me to gain hands-on experience delivering lambs and I also had to deal with common ailments associated with lambing, such as newborn lambs who are easily susceptible to infection and the prolapse of a ewe. My week on a dairy farm was particularly valuable as it allowed me to see the difference between small-animal veterinary medicine compared to a farm, where I assisted in routine procedures such as identifying White Line Disease in cow hooves, dressing wounds and blisters, learning the prevention and cure of mastitis and caring for calves. I was fortunate to witness a surgical procedure of a LDA on a heifer, allowing me to appreciate the physical strength and determination required by the vet. In comparison, working at a professional showing yard for horses allowed me to appreciate the high level of animal management, through balancing correct nutrition with the exercise required to produce an animal for the show ring, while ensuring the prevention of laminitis. By reading the *Veterinary Times* I am aware of current issues and news in veterinary medicine.

Through my varied work experience I have been able to appreciate the responsibility given to veterinary surgeons and others working with animals. As well as being given a degree of responsibility on my work experience, helping out at my local Pony Club camp for the past three years meant that I supervised the safety of 30 riders and their ponies; this also strengthened my communication skills by interacting with the children and their parents. Walking rescue dogs for three months as a part of my Duke of Edinburgh award allowed me to be responsible for dogs who had been ill-treated and taught me the importance of team work.

My hobbies include being a member of the school hockey team, a chamber choir, gaining Grade 8 in Singing and captaining the riding team for my college at the National School Equestrian Championships. Overall, my achievements in horse riding and music required me to have patience, determination and commitment, which I believe will be invaluable qualities in veterinary medicine.

I fully appreciate the responsibility, challenges and rewards associated with veterinary medicine and I believe that my academic ability, enthusiasm, determination and passion for animals will allow me to excel in this profession.

Notes on personal statement

- Interesting start.
- Range of work experience.
- Analysed skills gained on work experience.
- Good structure.
- A bit vague in places, such as *Veterinary Times*; would be better to use examples.
- Paragraph on extracurricular activities is a bit long; reads like a CV.

A 'perfect personal statement' is one that you are happy with. It is easier to say what makes a 'bad' personal statement than a 'perfect' one as 'perfect' is subjective. For example, there are always good points and bad points to a personal statement, as highlighted above; these examples were taken from successful applications, and yet there are still points to discuss. Remember: the statement needs to be an accurate reflection of you.

Bear in mind also that the clever personal statements will look at the course requirements, which are roughly the same for different universities, and discuss them in the personal statement.

General tips

- Do not copy anyone else's personal statement. There is no point as it will not reflect you. At the end of the day, you will only ever go wrong if you are not true to yourself. The clue is in the title: it is a 'personal' statement.
- Avoid quotes; these are your words, remember.
- Make sure you proofread your personal statement to check for careless errors; these may be easier to spot if you print off a copy before sending it off.
- Before submitting your application, ask someone else (for example, one of your teachers or a careers adviser) to check the statement for errors.
- However, do not get too many people to read it as, ultimately, everyone will have a different opinion as a personal statement is an individual reaction. It needs to be what you are happy with.
- Keep a copy of your personal statement so you can remind yourself of what you wrote, should you be invited to interview, and make sure you are happy and able to discuss all aspects of your statement, as this will form the basis of the interview.
- The best type of personal statement is one that interprets the experiences and relates them back to your learning.
- Unique experiences are ones that have developed you as a person and helped to confirm this course decision.

Advice from the admissions tutors:

'Really think why you wish to do this course. Too often people say the same thing over and over, which makes it hard to believe – so don't say you have wanted to do this all your life! If that is in fact true, what is more interesting is *why* you have wanted to do this for such a long time.'

'Please be very careful when footnoting anything that is shown on TV. It is not strictly accurate, and is often designed to make good viewing for the audience as opposed to showing the more routine elements of being a vet. If you are going to mention something, make sure it is for a purpose.'

'Referencing back to what you are learning at A level and how your knowledge has been useful in understanding the work you did is a very good way of writing your personal statement, and one students often miss.'

'Work experience is only useful to write down if you can explain what you learnt doing it, otherwise there is nothing we can take from it other than a list. We do put a good deal of emphasis onto work experience, so please be detailed as we have to compare personal statements against each other. It will also form the basis of some questions at interview.'

Fact: Horses use facial expressions to communicate with each other.

7 | So why did the chicken cross the road?

The interview

Once you've submitted your UCAS application, you must wait to hear from each of the universities you have applied to. If you meet their entry criteria and they feel that your application is strong in the areas they deem to be most important, they may call you for interview. The universities use interviews to find out first hand whether the picture painted by your application is accurate and to investigate whether you have the skills necessary to succeed on the course.

In this section, we will consider the different types of interview – multiple mini interview (MMI) and panel interview – and the steps you will need to go through in order to prepare, as well as more general interview pointers. Applicants might be invited to interview at any point between November and March, so it is important to start preparing as soon as your application has been submitted.

The purpose of the interview

The interview is designed to find out more about you. In particular, the interviewers will want to assess your motivation and the extent of your commitment to becoming a qualified veterinary surgeon, and so they may look to explore the following areas.

- Have you an appropriate attitude towards animal welfare?
- Are you reasonably well informed about the implications of embarking on a veterinary career?
- Are you a mature person possessing a balanced outlook on life?
- Do you have the ability to cope with the pace of what is generally acknowledged to be a long and demanding course?

To help them they will have your UCAS application, your referee's report and any supporting statements made by veterinary practitioners or people for whom you have worked. They will already have a good idea of your academic ability.

MMIs

The vast majority of interviews being conducted for veterinary medicine now take the form of MMI, with a shift away from the more traditional panel interviews.

The MMI is designed to judge the suitability of a candidate to study veterinary medicine. This style of interview question will have some similarities with the panel interview, but the major difference is that applicants participate in a number of small interviews and tasks with different interviewers rather than just sitting in one place answering questions with one set of people. These 'stations' will test a variety of abilities, ranging from academic knowledge to communication skills and logic and reason. The key is to remember that there are not always right and wrong answers – and most of the time, the interviewer is looking to assess how you deal with complex problems. The format of each station will vary, but you will receive instructions explaining what you will be required to do, so ensure that you listen carefully and read any written instructions to give you a good idea of what you will be facing.

There are two main reasons for veterinary schools using this type of interview. Firstly, research has suggested that traditional panel interviews give a poor indication of the likely performance of the interviewee as an undergraduate; the MMI improves on this. Secondly, one of the major criticisms of the panel interview is that students can be heavily coached on the vast majority of question types and, as a result, do not give an accurate indication of their personality and character attributes at interview. MMIs are therefore specifically designed to test those attributes of the interviewee in ways that are unlikely to be improved by participating in preparation courses, thereby allowing veterinary schools to build a better picture of the candidates' capabilities.

Some universities are relatively tight-lipped about the exact detail of the MMI and give little information to the interviewees, while others are more open to sharing the details of exactly what will be faced. You should pay close attention to any emails that you receive regarding the invitation to the interview, as well as carefully reading the interview section on the relevant university website.

Example of an MMI

We asked for the experiences of different students in their MMIs and their feedback was as follows:

Constructing a triangle

'The data sheet said to choose a correct length wire, bend it from 1.5cm at 60 degrees and the rest of the wire every 4cm with again 60 degrees to form the triangle shown, which was an isos-celes triangle with 1.5cm missing at one line of the triangle.'

Drug calculation

'They gave me the rates on how many moles of a specific drug should be used for a certain kilo of a dog. They then told me the weight of another dog and told me to calculate how much that one had to receive. They then gave how much mg/mole of that drug would be, so I had to calculate how many mg it would take to inject that dog. Then they said, under a certain condition, 40% less should be given to the dog and asked me to calculate how much he should then receive.'

Scenario-based

'They asked me what would I do if I was a veterinarian and some-one's cat died and they were really sad; so I had to role play this in order to tell them that their cat just died. They wanted to know how I would tell them the news. I talked about having empathy but not sympathy because I need to be able to see how they would feel but that I could not let myself feel as this might affect my performance with the rest of the animals.'

Scenario-based

'They asked me what would I do if one day I was walking with my dog in a forest near a road (and I wasn't using a leash) and all of a sudden he ran off somewhere and started barking. When I approached I saw that he was barking at a badger and I noticed that the badger wasn't able to move but I didn't know why.

'I talked about what the different factors were which might have caused the badger to become immobile and I said I would look to see if there were any shots on him as this might mean a farmer might have tried to kill him due to bovine TB; we then talked about the current issue of badger culling and that even though there was culling, it is now considered to be acceptable if it is done in a humane way in a cage. This wasn't the case, so I said I would make sure to let the police or the RSPCA (Royal Society for Prevention of Cruelty to Animals) know about the situation. I also said I would take my dog away immediately to protect him from TB. I knew that even though the question wasn't asking for it, they wanted a link with bovine TB and badgers.'

Data handing

'There was a table comparing three different things about pigs (their weight, how much they eat and how much money was spent on food) in three different farms (Farm A: normal farm,

> Farm B: top 30, Farm C: top 5). I had to then describe the graph. They then asked me which farm I thought was the best and why. Then they asked me how could Farm A improve (they were giving so much food to animals so they were spending too much money on food) and I said get food with higher nutrients instead so that less amount could still have enough energy.'

Panel interview

As discussed above, the traditional panel-style interview is being phased out by a number of veterinary schools in favour of the MMI. Although a panel interview is somewhat easier to prepare for due to the well-known nature of the potential questions, it can be very easy to fall into the trap of memorising pre-rehearsed answers. Some interviews have retained panel-style sections, and this gives you the opportunity to build rapport with the interviewers as you will spend more time discussing your application with a few people.

In the context of Covid-19, many interviews will be moved to online platforms for 2021 entry, making it more difficult to retain the MMI style in some cases. It is anticipated that some universities will revert to panel interviews while they are conducted online.

Preparation

Experience shows that personal qualities are just as important as academic ability, perhaps more so. The way you come across will be influenced by how confident you are, and thorough preparation can assist with this. This does not mean being overconfident. Many people believe that they can get through interviews by thinking on their feet and taking each question as it comes. This is probably an unwise attitude. Good preparation is the key. By being well informed on a variety of issues you will be able to formulate answers to most questions. There will always be the unexpected question for which no amount of preparation can help, but you can minimise the chance of this happening.

Confidence based on good preparation is the best kind, rather than the puffed-up variety that can soon be punctured by searching questions. While it is true that the interviewers will want to put you at your ease and will try to make the atmosphere informal and friendly, there is no doubt that there will be some tension in the situation. Think positively – this may be no bad thing, as many of us perform better when we are on our toes.

You should start your preparation by looking at your copy of the personal statement you submitted to UCAS. This is the most important part of your UCAS application and it should tell the interviewers a lot about you as a person, your work experience, your interests and skills. Many of the questions they ask will be prompted by what you have written in it. The questions will most likely begin with those designed to put you at your ease. As the interview proceeds you should expect them to become more searching. Try practising your answers to questions such as those shown below.

You should also be familiar with any additional information that you have provided, such as that on work experience forms that have been submitted. Interviewers may ask broadly about your work experience, but they may also ask for specifics, so keep a thorough record of what you have learned during your placements, as well as any key observations.

Questions to reflect on when preparing for interview

The questions discussed below should be considered regardless of the type of interview that you are attending. Although you will not be asked the majority of these questions in an MMI, preparing responses will help you to develop a real understanding of your reasons for applying and this will shine through in subtle ways in any interview.

Prior to the formal interview starting, you may be asked some generic, conversational questions. However, you shouldn't underestimate their importance – interviewers will be considering how you respond from the moment they meet you. They might also provide an informal manner of assessing how much you know about the university or the course.

Question: *Why do you want to study veterinary medicine?*

Comment: This is the question that all interviewees expect. Given that the interviewers will be aware that you are expecting the question, they will also expect your answer to be carefully planned. If you look surprised and say, 'Um ... well ... I haven't really thought about why ...,' you can expect to be rejected. Other answers to avoid are those along the lines of financial reward, or the fact that you come from a family of vets and are just following suit.

Many students are worried that they will sound insincere when they answer this question. The way to avoid this is to try to bring in reasons that are personal to you: for instance, an incident that sparked your interest (perhaps a visit to your local vets with a pet), or an aspect of your work experience that particularly fascinated you. The important thing is to try to express clearly what interested you instead of generalising your answers. Rather than saying 'being a vet combines science and working with animals' – which says little about you – tell the interviewers about the way in which your interest progressed.

You need to ensure that your answer is personal to you, but also honest. The interviewers may pick up on something that you said about work experience and ask you more questions about it. Since 'why do you want to be a vet?' is such an obvious question, interviewers often try and find out the information in different ways. Expect questions such as 'When did your interest in veterinary medicine start?' or 'What was it about your work experience that finally convinced you that veterinary medicine was for you?'

The answer will bring into focus your attitude to animals, the range of your work experience, those important manual skills, and your commitment to all the hard work entailed in studying to become a qualified professional veterinary surgeon admitted to the register of the RCVS.

Question: *Why do you want to come to this veterinary school?*

Comment: The interviewers will be looking for evidence of research, and that your reasons are based on informed judgement rather than just picking a university randomly from a list. Probably the best possible answer would start with, 'I came to your open day ...', because you can then proceed to tell them why you like their university so much, what impressed you about the university and facilities, and how the atmosphere of the place would particularly suit you. If you are/were unable to attend open days, try to arrange a formal or informal visit before you are interviewed so that you can show you are aware of the environment, both academic and physical, and that you like the place. If you know people who are at the veterinary school or university, so much the better.

You should also know about the course structure; the website will give detailed information. Although on the surface all veterinary medicine courses appear to cover broadly the same subjects, there are big differences between the ways in which courses are delivered and in the opportunities for patient contact, and your interviewers will expect you to know about their specific course.

Another useful source of information is the Unistats website (https://unistats.direct.gov.uk), which gives details of student feedback about each university and each course they offer. If there are particular areas that a university scores very highly on, these might be worth mentioning as a factor that has influenced your decision.

Answers to avoid are, for example, ones such as 'Reputation' (unless you know in detail the areas for which the veterinary school is highly regarded), 'I don't want to move away from my friends', 'You take a lot of retake students' or 'Someone said it was easy to get a place here'.

Question: *Tell us something about your work experience with animals.*

Comment: This question can arise in varying forms, such as, 'I see that you spent two weeks shadowing a vet in practice – was there anything that surprised you?', 'Was there anything that particularly interested you on your work experience?' or 'Was there anything during your work experience placements that you found off-putting?' What those questions really mean is, 'Are you able to show us that you were interested and engaged with what was happening during your work experience?'

This is one of the big questions of the interview. It would be surprising if the interviewers do not already have feedback from where you have been working. The interviewers will know what happens in a veterinary practice or on a farm, so lists of things that you saw or did will not shed any light on your suitability for the profession. Instead, concentrate on your reactions to the experience. Did you enjoy it? Were there any interesting or unusual cases that stick in your memory? Is your enthusiasm clear? Do you show your respect and sympathy for the animals? And what about the people – did you get on with them? The key phrases here are 'For example, when I …' and 'For instance, I was able to …'.

As previously discussed, you should keep a work experience journal to record all of your observations, as this will make careful reflection when preparing for your interviews more straightforward.

Question: *What are the main things you learned from your work experience?*

Comment: This is the typical follow-up question that gives you a chance to summarise and underline your impressions. You could try to indicate the varied nature of your experience and the different types of practice or farms you saw. There is also the business side of working with animals, for which you may not originally have been prepared. Maybe you were astonished at the responsibilities of the veterinary nurses. Be prepared to intrigue your listeners. A related question is: 'From your work experience, what do you think are the qualities necessary to be a successful vet?' Rather than answering 'Stamina, communication, physical fitness, problem solving …' and so on, bring in examples of things that you saw. For example: 'The ability to solve problems. For instance, when I accompanied a vet to a riding school, it was clear that one of the horses was very distressed, but it was unclear why …' and then go on to explain the steps involved in the diagnosis and treatment.

Question: *Have you ever felt frightened of animals?*

Comment: Vets shouldn't be frightened of animals, particularly small ones! However, honesty compels most of us to admit that we have at times and in certain situations felt vulnerable to a kick or bite. Explain the situation and what was said at the time – vets are noted for their humour! You could also reflect on the fact that increased exposure to animals through your work experience placements has enhanced your familiarity, and therefore your comfort in dealing with them.

Question: *What do you think of the TV programmes about vets?*

Comment: Nowadays, programmes specifically about vets in the UK are seen as less marketable than programmes such as those documenting wildlife abroad or those featuring celebrities such as Sir David

Attenborough: human nature is such that people are more interested by the exotic or the unknown. A few years ago there were several programmes on television following the everyday work of a vet. Such programmes were not always good for the professional standing of the vet. They made entertaining television, especially when they showed the animals and the caring 'honest broker' role of the vet between animals and humankind. They also almost universally presented vets as amiable people. On the other hand, though, you could argue that veterinary science was undermined when the programmes degenerated into 'soaps', with a portrayal of young vets whose work was an easy or incidental part of their lives. In your answer, show that you have thought about television's influence, and that you can recognise the realistic aspects but have also gained an insight into the less well-documented and ultimately less appealing side.

Question: *What do you think of rearing animals for meat?*

Comment: This type of question might be asked because it checks on your motivation. Perhaps you should start by looking at it from the animal's viewpoint. Animals should be kept well, with good standards of husbandry, and eventually slaughtered humanely. Of course, the animal does not know the reason for its slaughter, but you do. Some of your future clients may be farmers who make their living from supplying meat or poultry – what is your reaction? If you oppose eating meat, you should be honest but make it clear that you would be able to remain professional.

Question: *How do you feel about cruelty to animals?*

Comment: With the strong interest in and liking for animals that you would expect from all veterinary students, they will be watching your reaction. This is a question that you should expect and your response, while putting animal welfare first, should be strong and well-reasoned rather than too emotional. What would you do if you thought a farmer was acting in a cruel way to some of his livestock? Go to the police straight away? Talk over the difficulty with a colleague? Threaten the farmer by mentioning that you might bring in the RSPCA? The interviewers are not expecting you to come up with a perfect answer but rather to show that you are capable of coming up with a well-balanced and reasoned solution.

Question: *What are your views on euthanasia?*

Comment: They are looking for your ability to balance an argument. Any relevant examples would be helpful. Talk about it from the point of view of the animal and the owner. Do not be concerned about your own feelings as this is the job you wish to do and this is a regrettable part of it. Think of it from a humane point of view versus a human response. Also consider the implications of putting a horse down at the races (the Grand National for example) as there are obviously financial issues at play as well.

Question: *How important is the business element of veterinary medicine?*

Comment: Remember, some vets have to be business people as well. Smaller practices rely on the vets themselves to manage the practice. Therefore, you must be prepared to be strong when asking people for money, even in the face of tragedy for them. That can be hard, but the practice's survival is mostly based on your ability to recoup your charges.

Question: *Can you tell me about something that you have read recently in relation to veterinary medicine?*

Comment: If you are interested in making veterinary medicine your career, the selectors will expect you to be interested enough in the subject to want to read about it. Some good sources of information are the RCVS website (www.rcvs.org.uk), the British Veterinary Association (www.bva.co.uk) and news websites. You should get into the habit of regularly checking the news to see whether there are any veterinary- or farming-related stories.

Question: *How do you cope with stress?*

Comment: Veterinary medicine can be a stressful occupation. Vets have to deal with difficult people, especially when their beloved pets become unwell. Furthermore, there are few 'standard' situations: all animals are different, and they can each present with different problems. In these circumstances, the vet cannot panic but must remain calm and rational. In addition, the nature of the profession means that the financial aspects of running a business may also be a source of stress. The interviewers want to make a judgement as to whether you will be able to cope with the demands that the course and the job throw up. Once again, be sincere. Reflect on a particularly stressful time in your life and how you have coped through it. Remember, it is always best to use experiences from your own life than to talk generally.

Question: *I see that you enjoy reading. What is the most recent book that you have read?*

Comment: Although it may sound obvious, if you have written that you enjoy reading on your UCAS application, make sure that you have actually read something recently. Admissions tutors will be able to tell you stories about interviewees who look at them with absolute surprise when they are asked about books, despite reading featuring in the personal statement. The same advice is also true for any other interests you put on your personal statement: if you put it down, you need to be prepared to talk about it!

Question: *What interests do you have?*

Comment: Don't say 'Watch TV' or 'Go shopping'. Mention something that involves working or communicating with others, for instance sport or music. Use the question to demonstrate that you possess the qualities required in a vet. However, don't make your answer so insincere that the interviewers realise that you are trying to impress them. Saying 'I relax most effectively when I am shadowing my local vet' will not convince them.

There will, of course, be questions on your scientific knowledge and current topics (listed on page 115). Be prepared to answer many different types of questions, such as:

- What injections does a kitten require?
- Why haven't you got specific work experience in a particular area?
- Is training to help animals a good use of public money?
- If you have been to an abattoir (specifically for Liverpool), how do you slaughter an animal?

The Student Room (www.thestudentroom.co.uk) can be a good place to visit as students exchange their experiences and questions at interview. There are some great questions on there, such as, 'How lambs obtain immunity from their mothers and how that differs from humans'. It is very important to take what is written with a pinch of salt, though – it is a subjective forum and one person's experience is not the same as another's. You will see stories of tough and unfriendly interview panels in the same discussion thread as someone who found them to be very friendly. The message is: do not believe every horror story. More often than not, an interview panel is there to simply find out what you know, not to test you beyond your limits. Sometimes you will get questions that you do not know the answer to and in those situations you should feel confident in asking them to explain further and saying that you do not know, instead of trying to make the answer up. You can then have an informed discussion instead of them forming a view about you.

How to succeed in the interview

You should prepare for both types of interview as if you are preparing for an examination. Start by revisiting your personal statement as this is a common starting point for interviewers' questions. In particular, revisit the details of your work experience so that you can recount details of your time with a vet and reflect on the key experiences you had and lessons you learned. Then look through articles you have saved from the newspaper, the internet and magazines in relation to veterinary medicine, and consider all the things that you have mentioned in your personal statement. It is vital that you are truthful in your personal statement, as it is very easy to get caught out if you have lied.

When you are preparing for an interview, try to have at least one mock interview so that you can get some feedback on your answers. Your school may be able to help you. As mentioned previously, do not memorise set answers to questions; this is very easy to spot during an interview and will make you seem insincere. It is much better to have a good idea of roughly what you want to say and then put it across in a natural way. If possible, video your mock interview so that you are aware of how you come across.

At the end of your interview

In a panel situation you may be given the opportunity to ask a question at the end, although this won't happen in an MMI. Bear in mind that the interviews are carefully timed, and that your attempts to impress the panel with 'clever' questions may do quite the opposite. The golden rule is: only ask a question if you are genuinely interested in the answer (which, of course, is one you were unable to find the answer to on the website or when speaking to other people during your visit). Remember that the people interviewing you have lots to do and very little time to do it in, so most questions are better off asked to staff or current students that you meet at other points on the day of your interview.

Questions to avoid:

- What is the structure of the first year of the course?
- Will I be able to live in a hall of residence?
- When will I first have contact with animals?

As well as being boring questions, the answers to these will be available on the website. If you need to ask these questions, it will be obvious to your interviewers that you have not done any serious research.

Remember: if in doubt, don't ask a question. End by saying: 'All of my questions have been answered by the website and the students who showed me around the veterinary school. Thank you very much for an interesting day.' Smile, shake hands (if appropriate) and say goodbye.

General interview tips

As in any interview, appearance and body language are just as important as the answers you give to the questions you are being asked. The impression that you create can have a big impact. Remember that if the interviewers cannot picture you as a vet in the future, they are unlikely to offer you a place.

Body language

- Make eye contact with the interviewers, but don't stare at them!
- When you say hello to the interviewer, remember to smile.

- Sit up straight, but adopt a position that you feel comfortable in.
- Don't wave your hands around too much, but don't keep them gripped together to stop them moving either. Fold them across your lap, or rest them on the arms of the chair.
- Avoid annoying and repetitive body movements, such as jiggling your leg or tapping the table.

Speech

- Talk at your normal pace and beware of speaking too quickly. When you are nervous it is very easy to speed up your speech, so make a conscious effort to slow down if needed.
- Don't use slang or offensive language.
- Avoid saying 'Erm ...', 'You know', 'Sort of' and 'Like'. These are often said without one realising; another good reason to have mock interviews so that these habits can be highlighted to you.
- Say 'Hello' at the start of the interview, and thank the interviewer(s) and say 'Goodbye' at the end.

Dress and appearance

- Wear clothes that show you have made an effort for the interview. In reality, this should mean formal, smart dress. If you are unsure, it is better to be overdressed than underdressed with no way of making yourself look smarter.

How you are selected

During the interview, the interviewers (both MMI and panel) will be assessing you in various categories. Each interviewer follows careful guidelines to mark your performance so that they can compare each candidate fairly. The scoring system will vary from university to university, but you are likely to be scored in a number of categories, with the veterinary school setting a minimum mark that you will have to gain if you are to be made an offer.

If you are below the cut-off score but close to it, you may be put on an official or unofficial waiting list. If you are offered a place, you will receive an email from the veterinary school telling you what you need to achieve in your A levels: this is called a conditional offer. In addition, the conditions of your offer will be added to UCAS Track, although this can take some time, so don't worry if you are made to wait a while. Post-A level students who have achieved the necessary grades will be given unconditional offers in terms of the academic requirements, but may still be made conditional offers in relation to criminal record and health checks.

If you are unlucky, all you will get is a notification from UCAS saying that you have been rejected. If this happens, it is not necessarily the end of the road for veterinary medicine, as you may be able to reapply as a post-A level applicant. What you must do in this situation is contact the universities that you applied to and ask for feedback about why you were unsuccessful. Some universities will be more helpful than others and give relatively detailed feedback, which will give you points to consider, while others will just send a standard letter with no details about your particular application.

What happens next?

When UCAS has received replies from all of your choices you will then have a short period of time to make up your mind about where you want to go. If you have only one offer, you have two choices. One is to accept the choice and aim to get the grades to go to that university, happy in the knowledge that you are going to study the course of your dreams; the other is to reject the offer, if you have decided for whatever reason that you don't want to go to that university. If you choose to go down the latter route, you must then apply either the following year or add additional choices through UCAS Extra, although be aware that it is highly unlikely that places for veterinary medicine will appear on Extra.

If you have more than one offer, you must accept one as your firm choice, and may accept another as your insurance choice. If the place where you really want to study makes a higher offer than one of your other choices, do not be tempted to choose the lower offer as your firm choice and your preferred university as your insurance choice. You are obliged to go to the veterinary school that you have selected as your firm choice if you achieve the necessary grades. And even if you narrowly miss the grades required by your firm offer, you may still be accepted on the course; you would have to accept this offer so you would not be able to go to your insurance choice. You can go to your insurance choice *only* if your firm choice will not accept you.

If you receive no offers, there remains the option of completing a first degree and then attempting graduate entry, or reapplying the following year once your grades are in hand.

Case study

Grace has finished the third year of her veterinary course at the University of Bristol. She is 21 years old and is looking forward to beginning the fourth and fifth years of her training.

'I grew up in rural South Wales with lots of pets and always knew that I wanted to be a vet. I didn't take my GCSEs as seriously as I should have done but managed to get decent grades. I began to work hard when I started my A levels. After receiving top grades in biology, chemistry and mathematics, along with a strong BMAT score, I was offered places at both Bristol and Liverpool.

'I know everyone says the same thing, but what I learned from the process of applying for veterinary courses was the importance of work experience. After my GCSEs, I visited the careers adviser at my school who told me that these placements would be vital for my university application. I found it difficult to secure places at first, but after spending some time shadowing my family vet, she put me in contact with other local practices. I was also fortunate to live near a big working farm and they allowed me to help out each year during lambing season.

'I always knew that I wanted to be close to home for university so Bristol was the obvious choice. Although the first three years have been really hard work, I am really enjoying it and it has only reinforced to me that this is the career I want to pursue. I know the fourth year will be a challenge but I am looking forward to beginning my studies this year at the Langford campus.

'After speaking to others on my course, I know that I was lucky in my application and it isn't such a smooth process for everyone. I think the key is to prepare yourself and to take all opportunities that may help to give you a better knowledge of what it is to be a vet. It was great that in my university interviews I could answer confidently about the work experience that I had done, and I think this showed how passionate I am about following this career path.'

Topical and controversial issues

Your interviewer will want to find out whether you are genuinely interested in the profession, and alongside work experience, this includes testing your knowledge, awareness and appreciation of important issues: after all, if you are planning to devote the next 40 or so years of your life to veterinary science, you ought to be interested in issues that affect the profession. It could be about the diseases currently affecting the profession or the latest idea of dog pre-nups to safeguard the animal in situations of broken homes.

Most interviews last only 15 to 20 minutes, so there may not be time for questions of a more topical or controversial nature. Nevertheless, it may be worth investing a little thought into how you might sketch out an answer to questions covering one or more of the following issues, each of which will be outlined in this chapter:

- Ebola
- avian influenza (bird flu)
- bovine tuberculosis (TB) and badgers
- bluetongue disease
- canine influenza
- methicillin-resistant *Staphylococcus aureus* (MRSA)
- foot-and-mouth disease
- bovine spongiform encephalopathy (BSE)
- animal obesity
- canine lungworm
- swine influenza virus
- anthrax
- intensive farming
- fox hunting
- fall of dairy prices
- High Profile Breed List for dogs
- Dangerous Dogs Act
- hybrid dogs
- animal testing
- Covid-19
- antibiotic resistance
- Brexit.

This is not an exhaustive list but deals with the most current and topical issues in the veterinary profession. It would be worthwhile visiting www.gov.uk and www.dardni.gov.uk for a complete list of issues affecting animals in the UK.

Remember, most of the time there is no right or wrong answer for questions relating to issues such as these. It is really a case of demonstrating your understanding of an issue, your quality of judgement and your ability to discuss the issue clearly, logically and succinctly. A burst of enthusiasm and conviction won't do any harm either.

It goes without saying that the more informed you are, the more realistic your chance of entering this profession, so keeping up to date with recent developments affecting the veterinary profession is not only important but compulsory. The best sources of information are the broadsheet newspapers and internet news websites such as that of the British Veterinary Association (BVA: www.bva.co.uk). As well as the news sections, the health sections contain articles that will be of interest.

Check the news every day, keep a record of articles of interest, and store them so that you can revise from them before your interview. You will also find the Defra website (www.defra.gov.uk) extremely helpful. Other useful websites are listed in Chapter 12.

Questions on these issues are your chance to display a depth of knowledge from which you can open a discussion and show the clarity of analytical thought needed to be a vet. In many ways it is symptomatic of the profession and therefore good preparation. Good research ahead of your interview will also give you the confidence to feel able to discuss these issues with a professional.

At the time of going to print, the issues below are the most important current topics affecting the industry within recent years.

Ebola

The Ebola virus disease or EVD is an often fatal illness in humans. While not a strict veterinary issue, it is useful to understand how it originated. The virus is contracted from wild animals and is spread through human transmission. At present, the fatality rate is about 50%, according to the World Health Organization (WHO), but in the past that has reached 90%. Most recently, the disease was present in the Democratic Republic of Congo in early 2020. It is suspected that animals such as fruit bats are Ebola virus hosts and they spread it through the animal kingdom, passing it on to other animals. In turn, humans contract the virus when they come into contact with blood or other secretions from animals such as chimpanzees, monkeys, gorillas or forest antelope to name but a few. The WHO recommends that greater care should be taken when handling animals in that area, ensuring gloves and appropriate clothing are worn when handling any animal. Equally, meat should be well cooked.

Avian influenza (bird flu)

The first human case of avian influenza or bird flu was in Hong Kong in 1997. Before then it wasn't known that this type of illness could be passed from birds directly to humans. The virus is spread when infected birds excrete the virus in their faeces. Once this dries it becomes a powder and is therefore easily inhaled. Symptoms are similar to other types of flu – fever, malaise, sore throat and coughing. People can also develop conjunctivitis. All 18 people infected in 1997 had been in close contact with live birds in markets or on farms.

Countries known to have been affected by the disease include Cambodia, Indonesia, South Korea, China, Japan, Thailand, Vietnam and Hong Kong. Furthermore, since January 2004, human cases of avian influenza have been reported in Asia, Africa, the Pacific region and Europe. Avian flu has been seen to have a high fatality rate in humans. In 1997, six out of the 18 people who were infected died. In an outbreak in 2004, there were over 20 confirmed deaths.

There are 15 different strains of the virus, but it is the H5N1 strain that infects humans and causes high death rates. Even within the H5N1 strain, however, variations are seen, and slightly different strains are being seen in the different countries where there have been outbreaks of the disease. The H5N1 virus that emerged in Asia in 2003 continues to evolve and may adapt so that other mammals may be susceptible to infection as well. Moreover, it is likely that H5N1 infection among birds has become endemic in certain areas and that human infections resulting from direct contact with infected poultry and/or wild birds will continue to occur. So far, the spread of the H5N1 virus from person to person has been rare and limited.

Patients suffering from avian flu are often treated with antiviral drugs while researchers continue to work to develop a vaccine, though the difficulty is it develops into new strains over time. Currently, there is a ban on the importation of birds and bird products from H5N1-affected countries. The regulation states that no person may import or attempt to import any birds, whether dead or alive, or any products derived from birds (including hatching eggs), from the specified countries.

In January 2006, two children from the eastern Turkish town of Dogubeyazit, whose family kept poultry at their home, died having contracted the virulent H5N1 strain. Three months later, in the Scottish town of Fife, tests confirmed that a swan there had died from the deadly H5N1 strain of the avian flu virus. The discovery made Britain the four-teenth country in Europe to have the disease in its territory. The first major outbreak in the UK was in February 2007, on a turkey farm in Suffolk. In November 2008, the UK became free from avian influenza as defined by the rules of the World Organisation for Animal Health (OIE).

The AHVLA (Animal Health and Veterinary Laboratories Agency) conducts checks every year to determine whether avian influenza is present and publishes guidelines on www.gov.uk on how to spot it in birds. A strain of bird flu (H5N8) was found at a duck breeding farm in Yorkshire in 2014, though Defra ruled it low risk to public health. Bird flu was confirmed in poultry in Hampshire in February 2015, though it was the lesser H7N7 strain. Twenty-one days after infection, controls were lifted as the disease was contained and cleared. The last reported case of the more deadly H5N1 was in the first part of 2008. In 2016, a case of avian influenza was confirmed in Scotland in January of that year on a poultry farm. Restrictions were put in place around the farm, and were lifted in February after tests confirmed the disease to no longer be of concern at that time.

More recently, in 2020, vets and poultry keepers were advised to remain vigilant as Defra confirmed two cases of avian flu in England, with two different strains causing the infection – H5N2, a low pathogenicity strain was identified at a small commercial premises, and H5N8, a highly pathogenic strain, which was identified at a larger breeding facility. Wider testing since the identification of these strains has identified a spread to wild geese in several locations. As a result, an Avian Influenza Prevention

Zone was declared across England in November 2020 with additional bird housing measures put into force from mid-December 2020.

Bovine tuberculosis and badgers

Bovine tuberculosis (bTB) is a serious disease in cattle. Although the risk of tuberculosis spreading to humans through milk or meat is slight, it can be transmitted through other means, particularly to farm workers who have direct contact with the animals. The number of cattle slaughtered because of bTB has increased from 599 in 1986 to 37,655 for the year ending September 2020 across England and Wales.

There is uncertainty about the cause of the spread of bTB in cattle, but many people believe that it is passed on by badgers – a protected species. There is widespread support within the farming community for the culling of badgers, but this is opposed by wildlife and conservation groups. Over 20 years ago, in 1998, the government set up a badger-culling trial as well as taking steps to test the carcasses of badgers killed on the roads (about 50,000 every year) in order to try to find out more about the causes of the disease in cattle. However, the results were inconclusive, and the two opposing sides in the argument are still at loggerheads: the fundamental question remains unanswered – is bTB spread from badgers to cattle, from cattle to badgers, or is other wildlife involved?

Then, in November 2004, the government introduced enhanced testing and control measures to help improve the detection of bTB, so that action could be taken quickly to prevent the spread of the disease. A 10-year government strategic framework for the sustainable control of bTB in Great Britain was later published in March 2005. Through this framework, the government aimed to bring about a sustainable improvement in control of bTB by 2015. In December 2005, the government also announced pre-movement testing in England and Wales to help reduce the risk of bTB spreading between herds.

According to data, there was a reduction in the number of new bTB incidents in 2005 and again in 2006. Despite that reduction, however, levels of bTB remained high in comparison with other EU countries. On 7 July 2008, Hilary Benn MP, the then Secretary of State for Environment, Food and Rural Affairs, issued a statement to Parliament about bTB and badgers which declared that government policy was not to allow badger culling to control bTB for fear that the cull might make things worse. He went on to say that £20 million would be invested in vaccinations for badgers and cattle over three years. Mr Benn also intimated that he wanted to work closely with the farming industry to find an appropriate solution and, in conjunction with Defra, a Bovine TB Partnership Group was established. After the success of its work, in 2012, Jim Paice, the Agriculture Minister, announced a new Bovine TB Eradication Advisory Group for England which was to broaden into areas of conservation.

In this period, bTB was at its most prevalent. While Defra statistics showed a notable decrease in the incidence rate in 2012 in cattle, to 4.2%, compared with 6.0% in June 2011 (mainly as a result of an increased number of tests on unrestricted herds), cattle were, and are, still slaughtered in large numbers. Defra, however, advises that this figure of 4.2% should not be accepted as 100% accurate, as it included a number of unclassified incidents and there were further revisions made.

That said, the debate continues as there is huge resistance to the culling of badgers; opponents say that it risks increasing the spread of bTB instead of decreasing it. Leading experts on animal diseases say that, even if the increase does not materialise, culling is very unlikely to eradicate the spread of bTB. Many high-profile figures have joined the opposition at various stages, with Queen guitarist Brian May publicly lending his support, and several petitions to stop the cull have been signed and sent to Parliament.

From 2013, badger culls were undertaken to try to control the spread of this disease in pilot areas in west Somerset and west Gloucestershire. The secretary of state confirmed in 2014 that these licences would continue in the pilot areas; however, before the culls were to be rolled out in other areas, the process would be improved following a review into the humaneness of the operation. In June 2014, the number of new herd incidents was 2,398 compared to 2,535 in the equivalent period in 2013, with 17,063 cattle slaughtered.

In 2014, the government said it had achieved some degree of success with the policy mentioned above, laid out in 2005, and revised their target to become Officially Bovine Tuberculosis Free to 2038, within an interim objective of 'likely to be' in 2025 for large parts of the north and east of England.

In 2020, the government announced it had approved field trials of a groundbreaking cattle vaccine, which will be undertaken in two phases, with the second phase dependent on the success of the first. The success of these trials could lead to the end of badger culling, which currently takes place in 40 areas of England in an attempt to control the disease.

Bluetongue disease

Bluetongue is an insect-borne viral disease to which all species of ruminants are susceptible, although sheep are most severely affected. The UK has been officially free from the disease since July 2011; however, it is occasionally found in imported cattle and sheep, which must then be humanely culled. The most recent occurrence was in December 2018.

The disease is characterised by changes to the mucous linings of the mouth and nose and the coronary band of the foot. It was first described in South Africa but has since been recognised in most countries in the tropics and sub-tropics. Since 1999, there have been widespread outbreaks in Greece, Italy, Corsica and the Balearic Islands. Cases have also occurred in Bulgaria, Croatia, Macedonia and Serbia. It appears that the virus has spread from both Turkey and north Africa. One possible reason for the changing pattern of bluetongue disease in the Mediterranean region is climate changes. In September 2007, the first suspected UK case was reported in a Highland cow in Ipswich, Suffolk. Since then the virus has spread from cattle to sheep in Britain.

The clinical signs can vary from unapparent to mild or severe, depending on the virus strain and the breed of sheep involved. Deaths of sheep in a flock can be as high as 70%. Animals that survive the disease will lose condition, with a reduction in meat and wool production.

After bluetongue serotype 6 (BTV6) was confirmed on three farms in the Netherlands, on 20 October 2008 all exports from the Netherlands to other EU member states were banned as a precautionary measure while these cases were investigated. There are no reports of transmission to humans. On 5 July 2011, Great Britain was declared bluetongue free. While there are different strains of bluetongue virus, the important strain for Great Britain is known as BTV8.

In October 2014, Glasgow scientists made a breakthrough in adapting bluetongue vaccines to new strains of the disease. This is saving the industry millions, and was introduced nationwide in July 2016, as the BTV8 strain has cost the industry €80 million.

Canine influenza

Canine influenza refers to a strain of the influenza A virus that causes influenza in canines. It is a contagious respiratory disease that often has the same signs as kennel cough – sneezing, coughing and fever – and requires veterinary medical attention. The disease came to light in 2004 at a Florida racetrack when greyhound fatalities from respiratory illnesses were attributed to a mutated strain of the deadly equine influenza virus (H3N8) that has been detected in horses for over 40 years. Dogs have no natural immunity to this virus, owing to a lack of previous exposure, and therefore transmission rates between canines are recorded as being very high. Having affected the majority of American states, this specific strain of the influenza virus has now reached endemic levels. Statistically, roughly 100% of canines that come into contact with the virus – regardless of age or vaccination history – become infected. Of those infected, 20% show no signs of the virus. Of the 80% that exhibit signs, there have been two forms observed:

- mild infection – symptoms include a low fever, possible nasal discharge and a persistent cough for up to three weeks
- severe infection – symptoms include a high fever, increased respiratory rates, which lead to difficulty breathing, and potentially other indicators of pneumonia.

However, the more positive news is that research shows fatality in only 8% of infected canines, making it a disease with a high morbidity but a low mortality rate.

Canine influenza is believed to be a mainly airborne virus – i.e. it is transmitted by sneezing or coughing – with an affected dog able to spread the virus for seven to 10 days after contracting the strain. Symptoms will present within two to five days. It is also worth bearing in mind that infected dogs can spread the virus without exhibiting signs of disease in themselves.

Treatment of canine influenza will vary from case to case. Early symptoms may require only a course of antibiotics to stop any secondary bacterial infections, but more serious cases could require the same treatment that humans receive in influenza cases, i.e. fluids (supplied intravenously in severe cases) and rest. There is now a recognised vaccine to control both strains of canine influenza but it is not widely administered in the UK. The virus is not known to infect humans or poultry.

MRSA

Methicillin-resistant *Staphylococcus aureus* (MRSA) – or 'superbug' – is a major health concern for causing outbreaks in hospitals around the UK. Primarily affecting humans, as the BVA says, it may also colonise and cause infection in companion and farm animals. MRSA is of little risk to healthy animals and, although transmission of infection from animals to humans has been documented, the rate is thought to be low. The evidence available points to humans as the source of the MRSA strains.

Different strains of MRSA usually affect animals and humans. They are particularly adept at colonising and/or infecting their preferred host species. For example, the *staphylococci* that commonly infect and colonise dogs are usually from a different species, known as *Staphylococcus intermedius*, which differs in certain characteristics from *Staphylococcus aureus*. Although strains of the latter may have a preferred host species, they can opportunistically infect other species in some circumstances.

Reported cases of MRSA infection in animals can be traced back to 1999 and are often reported in the media, although there was an incident back in the mid-1980s regarding a cat that lived in a rehabilitation ward for the elderly. Since then, dogs, cats, rabbits and horses have all been diagnosed with the MRSA infection. This problem is not isolated to the UK, but is seen throughout the world, with cases reported in the USA, Korea, Japan and Brazil. There is evidence of pigs now being affected in the Netherlands.

Most MRSA infections, particularly in cats and dogs, have been post-operative infections, usually from wounds, though the numbers of skin, ear, urinary tract and bronchial infections have been lower recently.

There is evidence of a new strain affecting pigs and poultry but there is still no link with the human strain.

MRSA is a problem that will continue to trouble both humans and animals, because the effectiveness of antibiotics is constantly being challenged by the bacterium developing resistance to the drug.

Foot-and-mouth disease

The outbreak of foot-and-mouth disease (FMD) that occurred in February 2001 was the first in the UK for 20 years. Between February and September, 2,030 cases occurred. The previous major outbreak was in 1967, during which about half a million animals were slaughtered. Before the re-emergence of the disease, in a new and highly virulent form, it had been thought that FMD had been eradicated from western Europe. The latest form of the virus seems to have originated in Asia, and could have been brought into the UK in a number of ways. Something as trivial as a discarded sandwich containing meat from an infected source – brought into the country by, for example, a tourist – could have been incorporated into pigswill (pig feed made from waste food) and then passed on to animals from other farms at a livestock sale. The bovine spongiform encephalopathy (BSE) problem (see pages 123–124) led to greater regulation of abattoirs, which resulted in the closure of many smaller abattoirs. Animals destined for slaughter now have to travel greater distances and the possibility of FMD being passed to other animals is, as a consequence, greater.

The UK was declared FMD-free on 14 January 2002, almost a year after the first reported case. More than 4 million animals, from over 7,000 farms, were slaughtered during this period. The last recorded case occurred at the end of September 2001. The official report into the outbreak highlighted the lack of speed with which the government acted and that the understaffed State Veterinary Service (now called Animal Health) was unable to effectively monitor the disease. The disease took a month to diagnose and, by the time animal movement was halted, over 20,000 infected sheep had spread the virus across the UK.

There have been no outbreaks of the disease in the EU since the one in 2001, which affected not only the UK but also Ireland, France and the Netherlands. A Royal Society report recommended that vaccination – commonly used in a number of countries – should be a weapon in any future outbreaks. Vaccination is unpopular with some meat exporters since it is difficult to distinguish between animals that have been vaccinated and those that have the disease, and for this reason many FMD-free countries ban the import of vaccinated cattle.

FMD is a viral disease that affects cattle, pigs, sheep, goats and deer. Hedgehogs and rats (and elephants!) can also become infected, and people, cats, dogs and game animals can carry infected material. The virus can be transferred by saliva, milk and dung; it can also become airborne and travel large distances, perhaps as far as 150 miles. A vehicle that has driven through dung from an infected animal can carry the virus to other farms on its tyres. FMD is more contagious than any other animal disease, and the mortality rate among young animals is high.

The role of the veterinary surgeon in a suspected outbreak of FMD is not a pleasant one. If the existence of the disease is confirmed, the vet must make arrangements with Defra to ensure that all animals on the farm (and possibly on neighbouring farms) are slaughtered and then incinerated. For economic reasons, there is no question of the vet being allowed to try to treat infected animals.

The BVA has warned that 15 years on from the last big outbreak (it is worth noting there was a case in 2007), it is almost impossible to completely rule out the return of foot and mouth to this country.

Bovine spongiform encephalopathy (BSE)

BSE – commonly referred to as 'mad cow disease' – was first identified in 1986, although it is possible that it had been known about since 1983. It is a neurological disease that affects the brains of cattle, and is similar to scrapie, a disease of sheep that has been known since the 18th century. In 1988, a government working party stated that there was minimal risk to humans since, as scrapie was known not to spread to humans, so neither would BSE. It is believed that BSE originated in cattle as a result of the practice of using the remains of diseased sheep as part of high-protein cattle feed in an attempt to increase milk yields. In 1989, the government recommended that specific offal – such as the brain and the spleen – should be discarded rather than allowed to enter the food chain, and that diseased cattle should be incinerated. In the early 1990s, the increased incidence of Creutzfeldt–Jakob disease (CJD) – a disease similar to BSE that affects humans – caused scientists to look at the possibility that the disease had jumped species. At about the same time, scientists found increasing evidence of transmission between species following experiments involving mice, pigs and cats.

By 1993, there were over 800 new cases of BSE a week, despite the ban on animal feed containing specified offal. It became clear that the increase in the cases of CJD was related to the rise in BSE, and that it was likely that millions of infected cattle had been eaten before the symptoms appeared. In 1996, the EU banned the export of cattle, beef and beef products that originated in the UK. In 1997, the government set up a public inquiry. The findings were released in October 2000 and details can be found on www.encyclopedia.com/science/medical-magazines/bse-inquiry-report-executive-summary-key-conclusions. The total number of confirmed cases of BSE in Great Britain since 1986 is estimated to be about 185,000. There has been an overall decline in the epidemic in recent years, with only 16 cases between 2011 and 2018.

The BSE problem raised a number of issues concerning farming and food safety. In retrospect, the decision to allow the remains of diseased animals to be incorporated into feed for herbivores seems to have been misguided, at the very least. The problem with BSE is that the infecting agent, the prion (a previously unknown pathogen composed of proteins), was able to survive the treatments used to destroy bacteria and viruses. If any good has come out of the problem, it is that we are now much more aware of food safety. In April 2000, the government established the Food Standards Agency, created to 'protect public health from risks which may arise in connection with the consumption of food, and otherwise to protect the interests of consumers in relation to food'. Although it was established by the government, it can independently publish any advice that it gives the government, in order to avoid the accusations of cover-ups and secrecy levelled at the government over the BSE affair.

In March 2006, EU veterinary experts agreed unanimously to lift the ban on British beef exports, imposed 10 years earlier to prevent the spread of BSE. The closure of export markets had cost the British beef industry around £675 million.

In 2018, a case of BSE was confirmed on a farm in Scotland, which resulted in four animals on the affected farm being destroyed as per EU requirements. While causing alarm at the time, it highlighted the robust measures in place for BSE identification.

Animal obesity

Canine obesity has officially been classed as a disease. Researchers at the University of Glasgow have found that six out of ten pet dogs are overweight or obese, and independent research has shown that one in three household pets are overweight. Animals are putting on weight as a result of a number of factors, including being fed scraps from the dinner table, lack of exercise and even how old or rich their owners are.

Obesity can have a huge impact on an animal's health as it exacerbates a range of medical conditions, including arthritis and expiratory airway dysfunction, as well as affecting its lifespan.

This is a worsening problem, and a report from the PFMA (Pet Food Manufacturers Association) highlights that 77% of vets say that obesity has increased since 2009 in birds, cats, dogs and rabbits. This is despite guidelines and incentives being put in place for pet owners on portion size to exercise.

Canine lungworm

Angiostrongylus vasorum (or French heartworm) is a parasitic condition that is usually found in canines. Typically found in the heart and major blood vessels, lungworm causes many problems for the dog. If left untreated, it can cause fatal damage. Younger dogs are far more likely to be affected. The parasite is most often carried in slugs and snails and normally ingested by dogs eating these pests. Foxes are also to blame for spreading the disease around the country.

For anyone concerned about this, the signs to look out for are breathing difficulties, poor blood clotting, general sickness and changes in behaviour. While the main concern is obviously for the animal, as untreated it can be fatal, the spread of infection is a major issue. Canine lungworm is spread between canines through larvae in the faeces rather than directly, and so the worry is that dogs will become infected through close contact with the faeces of other dogs. Unlike roundworm, humans cannot become infected with this.

Swine influenza virus

This is a very common occurrence in pig populations: about half of the USA's pigs are thought to have the virus. While the swine flu outbreak of 2009 made the news in terms of its effects on humans, transmission of the virus from pigs to humans is relatively uncommon and does not always lead to human influenza, often resulting only in the production of antibodies in the blood. While it is uncommon, people with regular exposure to pigs are at increased risk of swine flu infection. If this causes human influenza, it is called zoonotic swine flu.

In pigs, three influenza A virus subtypes (H1N1, H1N2 and H3N2) are the most common strains worldwide. In the United States, the H1N1 subtype was the major strain pre-1998; after this time, H3N2 subtypes have been isolated from swine. As of 2004, H3N2 virus in pigs and turkeys contained human (HA, NA and PB1), swine (NS, NP and M), and avian (PB2 and PA) genes.

Transmission of the influenza virus is between infected and unaffected animals, with close transport, intensive farming and airborne infection all reasons for the spread of infection. Wild boar are considered to spread the disease between farms. The symptoms are sneezing, coughing, lethargy, decreased appetite and difficulty breathing.

As swine influenza is rarely fatal to pigs, little effort is made to treat the infection, with efforts instead being focused on stopping the spread of infection between farms. Antibiotics do exist, though, and are used to treat the symptoms of influenza.

Anthrax

Anthrax is a disease that can survive for centuries as the spores can live on through carcasses, hides and wool. It is then passed on through inhalation, ingestion or through lesions and breaks in the skin membrane. Anthrax is spread when its spores are inhaled, ingested or come into contact with skin lesions.

It affects mammals and also certain birds, but mainly cattle, sheep, horses and pigs. It can also affect humans. The risk of spreading to humans though is low. Cattle and sheep are likely to die quite quickly from the disease, even if they show no signs of it afterwards. The symptoms to be aware of are high temperature, shivering, blood in stool or nostrils, loss of milk, fits, colic, bright fixed expressions and loss of appetite. The symptoms are similar in horses and pigs, though they are likely to be affected by the disease at a slower rate. The only variation may be hot and painful swellings particularly in their throats, and while colic is likely to affect horses only, the loss of appetite is likely to be more prevalent in pigs.

In October 2015, in the first case in Great Britain since 2006, the anthrax disease was found at a farm in Wiltshire in two dead suckler cows. The farm had all movement restricted and the animal carcasses were incinerated. Defra encourages the practice of safe biosecurity on all premises with livestock in order to ensure outbreaks are minimal and contained.

Intensive farming

Meat and dairy products feature prominently in the British diet. Although carbohydrates (such as pasta and rice) comprise a greater proportion of our diet than they did 10 years ago, we still eat protein in higher quantities than is consumed by our southern European neighbours. We also demand cheap food. The meat, poultry, dairy and egg industries are faced with a choice – to use technological methods in order to keep the price of their products as low as possible, or to allow the animals that they farm to lead more 'natural' lives, which would necessarily reduce yields and increase costs. The use of drugs, hormones and chemicals is almost universal in farming (except in the organic farming movement), as are methods to control the movement of livestock by the use of pens, cages or stalls.

Intensive farming issues that concern the veterinary profession include:

- the welfare of live farm animals that are exported for slaughter
- battery farming of poultry
- the use of growth hormones
- humane killing of farm animals in abattoirs.

The Protection of Animals Act 1911 contains the general law relating to the suffering of animals, and agricultural livestock is also protected by more recent legislation. However, despite measures, figures released in 2020 indicate that large, industrial-sized pig and chicken farms in the UK have continued to rise in recent years owing to the demand for cheap meat. Since 2017, there has been a 7% rise in such units. With the arrival of Brexit, there is concern that new trade deals may result in greater competition between farmers to provide cheap produce. Currently, the Agriculture Bill does not set out to protect against this.

The veterinary profession is faced with a number of difficult decisions. It has to balance the pressure to produce cheap food with its primary aim of maintaining and improving animal welfare. An example of this is the use of antibiotics. Antibiotics are used in farming to treat sick animals. However, they are also used to protect healthy animals against the diseases associated with intensive farming and as growth promoters.

Antibiotic resistance

The problem with antibiotics is that bacteria become resistant to them, and overuse of antibiotics in animals has these serious effects:

- resistant strains of bacteria, such as salmonella and *Escherichia coli*, which can be passed on to humans, causing illness and, in extreme cases, death
- bacteria can develop resistance to the drugs that are used to treat serious illness in humans.

Antibiotic resistance is not a new concept and it is not a problem that is restricted to the veterinary sector, though the use of antibiotics within animal contexts has become increasingly problematic in recent years. Antibiotic resistance arises when pathogens, such as bacteria, develop random mutations that give rise to characteristics, such as the production of enzymes capable of hydrolysing certain chemical compounds, that are advantageous in the presence of a particular antibiotic by breaking them down and preventing them from working. These mutations arise independently of the presence of antibiotics, but when consistently utilised, or used on a widespread basis, such as on farms, these mutant bacteria have the opportunity to thrive, becoming the dominant strain. When this occurs, it can be extremely difficult to treat infections accordingly, leading to the widespread loss of animals, especially livestock. However, not using antibiotics in this way means that the infection, in its non-mutant form, can spread widely and devastate livestock regardless, making it a difficult situation to manage. As such, the current aim is to safeguard the use of existing antibiotics while new ones are produced to override the issues with resistance.

In order to deal with the issue of antibiotic resistance, a number of sector-specific targets have been set for their responsible use in the UK's food-producing animals over the next four years. To manage the progress towards these goals, vets will be heavily involved. Considerable progress has been made in recent years with a 75% reduction in the use of the highest priority critically important antibiotics (HP_ICAs) since 2014, putting the UK in the fifth lowest position of antibiotic use in food-producing animals in Europe.

To meet the targets of further reductions in antibiotic use by 2024, the focus is now on training vets in disease prevention rather than treatment. This could be achieved through improved vaccination programmes, which would eliminate the need for antibiotic use to the same extent.

Further information can be found on the BVA website at www.bva. co.uk/take-action/our-policies/responsible-use-of-antimicrobials.

Fox hunting

While not necessarily an issue concerning vets, it is certainly something that you should have an appreciation of as it does concern the animal world. Most people have a view on the issue of hunting with hounds. Prior to the Hunting Act of 2004, there were those, on the one hand, who argued that fox hunting was an integral part of rural life and a countryside tradition, that foxes kill farm animals and therefore need to be controlled, that thousands of rural jobs would be lost if it were banned, and that a ban on fox hunting would lead to a ban on other pastimes, such as shooting and fishing. On the other hand, many people believed that it was a cruel and unnecessary way to control foxes, claiming that around 20,000 foxes were killed every year and that about half that number of hunting dogs were also killed taking part in the sport. Animal rights activists believed it was immoral to chase and kill animals for sport.

The Hunting Act 2004, which banned fox hunting in England and Wales, took effect in February 2005. The Act makes it an offence to hunt a wild mammal with a dog. Nevertheless, some forms of hunting are exempt, including those using no more than two dogs to flush out a mammal to be shot. Controversy on what is a very emotive subject therefore still remains. On the first anniversary of the ban, in February 2006, hunt supporters called for the Act to be repealed, while the League Against Cruel Sports accused 33 hunts of repeatedly breaching the law.

For opposing sides of an argument which continues to be pursued, you should investigate the websites hosted by the League Against Cruel Sports (www.league.org.uk) and the Countryside Alliance (www.countryside-alliance.org). The Conservative Party committed to not changing the 2004 Act in its 2019 general election manifesto.

Fall in dairy prices

The UK is the ninth largest milk producer in the world and the third largest in Europe. Although largely (90%) self-sufficient in milk, the UK participates in a significant trade in dairy products. Nevertheless, farmers' unions are warning that the UK dairy industry is facing meltdown unless a national dairy body is established that can regulate farm-gate milk prices.

Milk prices have been low for a number of years and this has been reflected in dairy farm incomes. As a consequence, some dairy farmers are leaving the industry. One in three dairy farms were forced to close between 2013 and 2016 as a result of supermarkets introducing 'mega dairies', as it is cheaper than paying dairy farmers; that is a closure of nearly 1,000 dairy farms. However, new regulations following Britain's departure from the EU is likely to cause dairy prices to surge due to the complexity of exporting products.

High Profile Breed (HPB) List for dogs

The Kennel Club is an organisation that advises on issues such as buying and breeding dogs and how best to keep them at home. It also acts as a lobbying committee for issues within the dog world if it believes that tougher action is required to prevent actions that put dogs at risk. In recent years, the European Convention Study Group/2002, set up by the Kennel Club, has identified a number of 'high-profile' breeds of dog, which it defines as:

> 'A breed from time to time designated by the General Committee as requiring particular monitoring by reason of visible condition(s) which may cause health or welfare concerns.'

These breeds are usually added because someone, whether that be a member of the general public or a professional, has expressed concerns about the health or welfare of the animal. Once the concerns have been identified, the Kennel Club looks closely at the key issues to be addressed within the breed and at health surveys and reviews of the animal, and gets expert opinions on the animal's welfare. The Kennel Club then advises breed clubs on those issues and provides guidance on effective steps to be taken.

At the moment, the ten dogs identified in the HPB List are:

- bloodhound
- bulldog
- dogue de Bordeaux (DDB)
- German shepherd dog (GSD)
- mastiff
- Neapolitan mastiff
- Pekingese

- Pug
- St Bernard
- shar pei.

In order to remove a dog from the HPB List, breeders should submit a proposal for their breed to be removed from the list. The committee looks at the recent health survey of the breed, a programme for the ongoing health of the breed, a report from a veterinary surgeon, supporting material from breed clubs, reports and quantitative data with specific veterinary comment, among other things. A formal re-evaluation takes place three years after removal.

Dangerous Dogs Act

The Dangerous Dogs Act, which was introduced in 1991, banned the ownership, breeding, sale and exchange and advertising for sale of specified types of fighting dogs. The dogs covered by the ban included the pit bull terrier. The Act was amended in 1997, one of the effects of which was to lift the mandatory destruction orders that courts applied to dogs found to be of those types listed in the Act. It is now possible, therefore, for prohibited dogs to be added to the Index of Exempted Dogs, but only at the direction of a court and only if the necessary conditions are met (tattooing, microchipping, etc.). No owner may apply to have their dog added to the index – it is entirely a matter for the courts to decide upon. The maximum penalty for illegal possession of a prohibited dog is a fine of £5,000 and/or six months' imprisonment.

Should this issue arise at interview, it is important to demonstrate that you are aware that vicious attacks by certain breeds of unmuzzled dogs on children and adults led to the Act requiring owners to register such dogs with the police and to keep them muzzled.

For the qualified vet, controversy might arise if they are called on to destroy, for example, an unmuzzled pit bull terrier before it has committed an offence. Is such action contrary to the professional oath of a veterinary surgeon? (Privately, many vets say that the Act is unworkable.) If you take a view on this in an interview you will get credit for at least knowing about the law, whether the interviewer agrees with your conclusion or not.

Hybrid dogs

In a consumer-focused society, designer dogs – from labradoodles to puggles – have become the new fad. But does this pose any danger? Originally these designer dogs were designed as a hypo-allergenic version of the guide dog, but the issue of hybrid breeds throws up an ethical question. Hybrid dogs are now sold for staggering amounts of money, and it does raise questions of what hope is there for the adoption of other dogs and for rescue shelters. However, the advantage of breeding designer or hybrid dogs can often be a reduction in the level of genetic defects or health problems found in particular breeds of pedigree dog. The hybrid dog has a much larger genetic pool and therefore a lower risk of suffering from the same health problems of either one of its parents. Hybrid dog breeding remains a controversial topic but one that you should know about and be happy to comment on in terms of both advantages and disadvantages.

Animal testing

Almost all of the drugs used to treat humans have been tested on animals. Without rigorous and controlled testing, there are significant health risks associated with the use of new medicines. In many cases, the long-term or side effects of drugs can be more serious than the illness itself, and testing is therefore essential. Lord Winston, who pioneered in vitro fertilisation (IVF) and went on to become a household name through his BBC television series *The Human Body*, in response to a report by the House of Lords Select Committee on Science and Technology was quoted in the *Independent* as saying: 'Perceived pressure may persuade people to go down a route which is not going to promote human welfare. We have a major job – animal research is essential for human welfare. Every drug we use is based on it. Without it those drugs would be unsafe.'

Each year British laboratories experiment on approximately 3 million animals. British law requires that any new drug must be tested on at least two different species of live mammal, one of which must be a large non-rodent. UK regulations are considered some of the most rigorous in the world – the Animals (Scientific Procedures) Act 1986 insists that no animal experiments be conducted if there is a realistic alternative.

The debate on animal testing has become a high-profile one because of the activities of animal rights groups. Although the majority of animal rights groups campaign peacefully, the newspapers have given a good deal of publicity to a number of attacks on research laboratories. Opposition to animal testing is centred on the idea that if animals are similar enough to us for test results to be meaningful, then they are too similar to be experimented upon. Conversely, drugs tested on animals have also gone on to have devastating effects on humans. Examples are the drugs thalidomide and sodium valproate, and the drug trial in March 2006 that caused six men to have multiple organ failure. Campaigners argue that there are alternative methods of testing that do not involve animals. Many of these methods are, they say, also cheaper, quicker and more effective. They include:

- culture of human cells – this is already used in research into cancer, Parkinson's disease and acquired immune deficiency syndrome (AIDS)

- molecular methods, including DNA analysis
- use of micro-organisms
- computer modelling
- use of human volunteers.

The Covid-19 pandemic

While the extent of the transmission of Covid-19 between animals and humans has not yet been fully elucidated, it is thought to have originated in bats in the Wuhan province of China before causing infection in humans, leading to the pandemic and its consequences, which we are all now so familiar with. The veterinary sector has not been exempt from its impacts; while veterinary practices were able to stay open, they were advised to minimise their procedures as much as possible.

It is no secret that working as a vet is extremely stressful, but concerns rose amid the Covid-19 pandemic as pressures mounted. In a survey conducted by the British Veterinary Association, three-quarters of vets stated that they were concerned about stress and burnout as a consequence of the pandemic six months after it took hold in the UK. Their major concerns were:

- stress and burnout in the profession
- the provision of EMS for vet students
- confidence of veterinary students and new graduates
- the impact of a recession on the veterinary sector and job security
- animal health and welfare in wildlife and zoos in the medium term
- contracting Covid-19 in the workplace.

By reducing the number of animals they were able to see, the number of treatments they were able to carry out (i.e. only those regarded as emergencies), and the number of staff they were able to have on the premises at any one point in order to adhere to social distancing guidelines, veterinary practices would have undoubtedly suffered financially.

The impact of Covid-19 on animals appears to be relatively negligible at the moment. Only a small number of domesticated animals have tested positive for the virus worldwide, with minimal or no clinical symptoms. Those that did present with symptoms prior to testing had minor respiratory and gastrointestinal distress. However, on 22 July 2020, a domestic cat tested positive for Covid-19, and while there was no evidence of the cat being involved in transmission, it inevitably led to a series of concerned pet owners contacting their local veterinary practices and requesting tests for their pets, especially if they themselves had tested positive for the virus. Despite the growing concern, Public Health England did not recommend routine animal testing, and advised that humans conducted regular handwashing, especially when in contact with animals.

While the impact on domestic animals has been inconsequential thus far, a mutated version of the virus infected millions of farmed mink in Denmark. As hundreds of people became infected with the mink-related version of the virus, parts of the country were forced into lockdown and a mass culling of mink was ordered over fears that widespread infection with the variant form of the virus could undermine any vaccination efforts. The original virus, which mutated to be able to spread from bats to humans, was passed into mink from infected farm workers before undergoing further mutation to transmit back into people. Concerns rose as the particular mutation that had arisen in mink affects the spike protein, found on the surface of the virus, which has been a target of various vaccination developments. At the time of writing, the World Health Organization has reported that these early findings are concerning, but that the significance it might have on vaccination programmes and treatment moving forward were as yet undetermined. Their advice, at this point in time, has been for mink farms to tighten biosecurity and surveillance, remaining vigilant for signs of a potential outbreak. It is worth noting that while there is no evidence that this particular strain of the virus is any more dangerous in humans than the existing versions, the incident does highlight the significance of zoonotic pathogen transmission.

Brexit

The UK's departure from the EU in January 2021 may impact several aspects of the vet profession. One of the biggest potential issues to surface is the UK's considerable overreliance on abattoir vets from the EU, who account for over 90%. Abattoir vets are critical for ensuring that animals are slaughtered in a manner that is as humane as possible, and there are significant concerns that with a loss of EU vets working in such roles, animal welfare standards could fall. However, ministers have insisted that welfare and environmental standards will be maintained. However, there are concerns that these standards might ultimately be watered down, which would have an impact on food safety and hygiene as a result. It is hoped that the UK government will guarantee working rights for EU resident vets working in the UK in order to minimise the impact of the veterinary profession generally, but especially in the context of abattoirs which will be hit most heavily.

Another concern is that following the UK leaving the EU, access to veterinary medicines might be difficult due to restricted imports of pharmaceuticals licenced through EU regulatory systems. Similar concerns have been echoed throughout the NHS, meaning that this area of concern has already achieved significant attention.

More broadly, there are concerns regarding trade, research and development (and partnerships with EU institutes), food hygiene and safety, veterinary medicines, animal health, animal welfare and the veterinary workforce. The British Veterinary Association has summarised the major concerns in its Brexit and the Veterinary Profession document (www.vin.com/apputil/image/handler.ashx?docid=8340035).

Other issues

In addition to the topics listed above, it is advisable for an aspiring vet to have some prior knowledge of other issues that have affected the profession over the past decade. You are also strongly advised to check out the Defra website and look at some of the other global issues affecting animals today, such as African horse sickness, koi herpes virus and West Nile virus.

In the interests of complete exposure, below are note summaries of the current diseases as listed by the World Organisation for Animal Health and Defra. It is not necessarily important that you know about Brucellosis, or even Rift Valley fever, but it is worthwhile having a superficial understanding of them. Visit the World Organisation for Animal Health, at www.oie.int/animal-health-in-the-world/oie-listed-diseases-2020 and Defra's notifiable diseases, www.gov.uk/government/collections/notifiable-diseases-in-animals.

African horse sickness, affects horses, does not affect humans; there has never been an outbreak in the UK.

African swine fever, affects pigs, does not affect humans; there has never been an outbreak in the UK.

Aujeszky's disease, affects pigs and is sometimes called by pseudo-rabies. It has also been known to affect cattle, sheep, cats, dogs and rats. The last known outbreak in Great Britain was in 1989. It is a nervous system condition and is fatal for piglets.

Brucellosis, there are several different types affecting different animals, it does not affect humans; there was an outbreak in Great Britain in 2004 and it affected cattle.

Chronic wasting disease, affects deer, it has been devastating in northern America and Canada but it is not known to affect humans; there has never been an outbreak in the UK.

Classical swine fever, affects pigs, it does not affect humans; the last outbreak in the UK was in 2000.

Contagious agalactia, affects sheep and goats, it does not affect humans; there has never been an outbreak in the UK.

Contagious bovine pleuro-pneumonia, affects cattle, it does not affect humans; there has not been an outbreak in the UK since 1898.

Contagious epididymitis, affects sheep and goats, it does not affect humans; there has never been an outbreak in the UK.

Contagious equine metritis, a disease in all types of equine animals and is usually spread during mating, it does not affect humans; the last known case in the UK was in 2012.

Dourine, a disease in all types of equine animals, it does not affect humans; there has never been an outbreak in the UK.

Echinococcus multilocularis, a tapeworm that affects foxes and other canids, including domestic dogs, and can cause serious illness in humans; there have been no known domestically acquired cases in the UK.

Enzootic bovine leukosis, affects cattle, spread during pregnancy, during suckling or by animals grouped together; it does not affect humans and the last outbreak in Great Britain was in 1996.

Epizootic haemorrhagic disease, generally considered to affect all animals that chew cud, does not affect humans; there has never been an outbreak in the UK.

Epizootic lymphangitis, principally affects horses and mules (also can affect cattle but that is rare), it is spread by flies and contamination on equipment, it does not affect humans; the last case in Great Britain was in 1906.

Equine infectious anaemia (swamp fever), spread by horse flies, this only affects horses, causes tiredness and fever in the animal, it does not affect humans; the last known case in Great Britain was in 2012.

Equine viral arteritis, spread through mating, this affects equine animals but is only notifiable in stallions and mares, it does not affect humans; the last known case in Great Britain was in 2012.

Equine viral encephalomyelitis, affects horses, donkeys, mules, zebras, cattle, sheep, goats, pigs, birds, dogs, rodents and humans; there has never been an outbreak in the UK.

Glanders and farcy, transmitted through ingestion, either eating or drinking, it affects horses, donkeys and mules, and can also be 'chronic', often lasting for years; it is potentially fatal for humans, with the last case in Great Britain being in 1928.

Goat plague, affects goats and sheep, does not affect humans; there has never been an outbreak in the UK.

Lumpy skin disease, it affects cattle and water buffalo, does not affect humans; there has never been an outbreak in the UK.

Newcastle disease, affects poultry, captive and wild birds, it is spread through the exchange of bodily fluids and it can be harmful to humans, though only in the short term and does not require treatment every time; the last reported case in Great Britain was in 2006.

Paramyxovirus infection, spread as a result of unsanitary conditions for pigeons, it affects the pigeon population and it is not known to be harmful to humans; it is currently a disease present in Great Britain and worthwhile researching.

Porcine epidemic diarrhoea, otherwise known as 'PEDV' and highly infectious, it affects pigs and is currently posing a significant risk to British herds; it does not affect humans.

Rabies, affects all mammals, transmitted in infected animals' saliva and through their bite and can affect humans. The important thing is to look for a change in behaviour in the animal as rabies manifests itself in an animal in different ways; it was eradicated from all mammals in the UK in 1922 but it still exists in bats. A risk is still posed to humans if they are bitten or scratched by a bat.

Rabies in bats, as above but note that the most recent case of rabies in bats in the UK was in July 2020.

Rift Valley fever, affects sheep, goats, cattle, lambs and humans; there has never been an outbreak in the UK.

Rinderpest, a disease that affects cattle, spread through direct contact and exchange of bodily fluids, although there is no risk to humans; the last known case in Great Britain was in 1877 and it was eradicated from the world stage in 2011.

Schmallenberg virus, most commonly transmitted by midges, mosquitoes and ticks, it causes mild to moderate disease (milk drop, pyrexia and diarrhoea) in adult cattle and late abortion or birth defects in newborn cattle, sheep and goats; it is currently present in Great Britain in isolated cases. There is a low risk to public health.

Scrapie, affects the brains of sheep and goats and is fatal. Two types, classical and atypical, the former being highly contagious, the latter being barely contagious, as a result of which, most of the advice around scrapie is to do with the animal husbandry. If found, often this will lead to a cull of the flock; it has not been proven to affect humans; it is active in the UK.

Sheep and goat pox, as implied, only these animals are in danger of this disease, spread usually through direct contact or insects; there has not been a case in Great Britain since the 1800s.

Sheep scab, a skin condition in sheep alone, passed on by mites through direct contact of the fur; it is very much present in Great Britain today but poses no immediate fatal risk.

Swine vesicular disease, affects pigs, and while it is not common in humans, there have been incidents that have shown that it can accidentally pose a risk to human health. It will mostly be spread through faeces and bodily fluid or by pigs eating infected meat or something else; the last case in Great Britain was in 1982.

Teschen disease, affects sheep, does not affect humans; there has not been a case in Europe since the 1980s. A less severe form of the disease called Talfan has occurred in the UK.

Vesicular stomatitis, affects cattle, horses, pigs and donkeys, sheep and goats can also be affected but they are more resistant, it does not affect humans; there has never been an outbreak in the UK.

Warble fly, normally affects cattle but also can affect deer and horses too, spread via insects, it does not pose a risk to human health; the disease has not been seen in Great Britain since the 1990s.

West Nile fever, affects many types of animals from cattle to horses, it also affects humans as it is mostly spread by mosquitoes. The symptoms are often a lack of energy and swollen lymph nodes, usually in the neck; birds tend to carry the disease between countries when they migrate; while it is not rife in Great Britain there are some cases to note.

Source: 'Notifiable diseases in animals' (www.gov.uk/government/collections/ notifiable-diseases-in-animals#history). Contains public sector information licensed under the Open Government Licence v3.0.

Case study

Having grown up around horses, Marie had always had her sights set on being an equine vet. She went on to qualify as a veterinary surgeon after studying at the University of Bristol, but her specific plans changed after she adopted two corn snakes and got hooked on exotics! Having completed some placements in exotics practices and zoos, she knew this was the path for her, and she now works as an exotics and zoo vet.

'After graduating, I started off working in a small-animal and exotics practice that supported me to be competent and confident with consulting, surgery and working with both domestic and exotic animals. The first year was a steep learning curve, but I enjoyed it for the most part, and had some good colleagues to lean on when I needed them. After 18 months, a residency in avian medicine became available in a referral hospital. These specialist training positions are rare, and although I wasn't necessarily excited about birds, I knew this was one of very few chances to get that training. I applied and got the position. I then spent three years specialising, with a high bird caseload that I grew to enjoy, but also a wide range of other exotic animals. I did placements in pathology, ophthalmology, surgery, medicine and did night shifts with small animals as well as the day-to-day work. I completed my certificate in zoo medicine at the same time.

'After my residency, I moved to Birmingham and set up an exotics and zoo department in a practice group, which expanded rapidly and is still thriving. I completed my diploma in zoo and wildlife medicine while there and became an accredited specialist. After six years, I was struggling to run a large, busy department and keep up with being a parent and having a life outside work, so switched to consultancy work. I spent a couple of years as a visiting specialist to various zoo collections and practices, wrote articles, took on RSPCA cases with exotics animals and started writing a textbook on exotic animal medicine and surgery. I enjoyed a bit more freedom and flexibility to pick and choose what I wanted to do and when I was going to do it. However, when a full-time zoo job came up locally I couldn't resist it; I went on to spend three years working with a huge range of species, from invertebrates to rhinos. I also finished my textbook, in the brief moments around work and life! I now work part time for an exotics practice, continuing consultancy work and writing around this.

'My current role is as head vet for an exotics practice, consulting and operating for three days a week and covering emergencies. The days are long and very busy, but I enjoy having a hands-on role and being able to build up relationships with clients and pets, and investigate and treat cases to a high standard. We work with zoo collections as well as private keepers, so the patients vary greatly and I love the unpredictability and the range of skills needed to successfully handle and treat them. I have a range of interests, including reptile surgery, invertebrate medicine, reproductive management in zoo mammals and legal work.

'The most rewarding part of the job is that I can actually make a difference to an animal or their carer's day, or even life. It is a very tough job a lot of the time, and there are some harder days, but at the end of the day being able to get home, put my feet up and reflect on what we have achieved is a good feeling. I still see new things, and love the feeling of finding out something new, completing a new or challenging surgery, and seeing an animal that was struggling back to full health.

'There is a huge weight of expectation on vets to be able to fix animals immediately and with cost limitations. With exotic patients these issues are often compounded by the lack of knowledge available for many species and disease processes, so there is a constant learning process and daily challenges. Financial restrictions are also more common with many exotic and zoo animals, so trying to reach a diagnosis and cure can be a careful balancing act, and as a profession we are not good at accepting defeat and take personal responsibility for not achieving success regardless of limitations that have been placed on us.

'There is a growing acceptance that the way vet practices work is not good for the mental and physical health of vets – 12-hour days, being called in overnight and on days off, a constant stream of new patients with restricted time to deal with them, higher pet-owner demands (and increased social media expression of malcontent) – plus greater financial pressures and lack of support have led to the loss of many good vets from the profession. I have been lucky that I have been in positions where I was able to control my work to a reasonable degree, and walk away when conditions weren't working, but I have seen the pressures exerted on colleagues and the detrimental effects. The recognition that this is not a constructive way to work is a big step forward, and working conditions are slowly changing for the better.

'If you are an aspiring vet, be prepared to work incredibly hard, not only for exam results and to gain experience now, but through-out the degree and in working life, especially that first year when everything is new and scary. Make sure you have a good support network of friends and family who are happy to provide tea, cake and listen to you vent when you've had a rough day. It is a career that is going to push you to your limits repeatedly, but it's also a profession where you are surrounded by people that understand your battles, will help you wherever they can and be like a family you never expected!

'Oh, and be prepared to end up with a house full of stray or slightly wonky pets that had nowhere else to go!'

Importance of the interview

So, those were just a few of the possible questions and issues that you might expect to come up at a selection interview for entry to veterinary school. To be called for interview is a positive sign as it indicates that your application is being considered, and a good interview can lead to an offer. Another reason for trying to do well at the interview stage is that candidates whose grades fall just below those required in their conditional offers are often reconsidered. If places are available, a good interview performance could tip the balance in your favour.

Advice from admissions tutors

'Be yourself, as the only way to control your nerves is when you are in control of yourself. We want to meet you. Try and remember we judge you on your body language too so how you come across is important, simply because it will be important when you are actually a vet facing clients.'

'Read your personal statement thoroughly. I lose count of how often students cannot refer back to what they wrote in answers they give to us and it is not our job to spoonfeed you.'

'We are not trying to catch you out, but we are trying to get you to think. Questions can and will be varied but all will be answerable. Some might seem harder than others; however think about what the question is actually asking you and try and give an answer based on that. The key is balance, giving both sides to the argument. If you do not know the answer to a question, please just say that and we will help you. Do not make something up as you will tie yourself in knots. If you would like the question clarifying, please ask as this will not be a detrimental factor in your interview.'

'Practice is important, and you can clearly notice the difference between those who have put in the effort in advance and those who have not. Do not over-prepare as no one wants robotic answers, rather ask fellow applicants and tutors to throw questions at you and make sure they are different each time.'

Fact: Dogs can alert their owners of an epileptic seizure up to an hour before it occurs.

8 | A leopard does not change its spots

Non-standard applicants

This book has focused on those students who are applying on a 'standard' application – typically UK residents studying A levels, IB, Highers or the Irish leaving certificate for example – but these are not the only qualifications. If you do not meet the 'standard' applicant profile, there are other possible entry routes that can be pursued.

Overseas students

The competition for places at veterinary school is high and, as an overseas student, it would be sensible to email an admissions tutor to discuss your application informally with the university before submitting it. If you have not taken A levels or the International Baccalaureate (IB), this does not mean that you will not get a place. However, you do need to have a qualification recognised by English institutions and you need to refer directly to the universities with your specific qualification for advice. Information about qualifications can also be obtained from British Council offices in your country (www.britishcouncil.org). The UCAS website also has a section for international students which describes in detail the application process and deadlines.

Following the UK's decision to leave the European Union in 2016, students who are resident in the EU outside of the UK will be classified as overseas students for application and fees purposes from September 2021.

Fees

Overseas students are liable for the full cost of tuition, as they are not eligible to access the funding available to domestic students. Fees for international students, including those from the EU from 2021, are not capped at £9,250 per year and generally exceed this. Universities do have international scholarships available however, and it is always worth researching these in order to access financial support where required. For these you apply directly to the university. See Chapter 10 for more information on fees and funding.

English language qualifications

In order to prove your English ability you must pass an English language test. This is for any student who is not a British citizen. The most common test is the IELTS (International English Language Testing System). You should be looking at achieving at least IELTS 7.0 in order to begin the university course and certainly no less than 6.5 in each band, though you should check each university's policy carefully as there are some minor deviations from this standard set of scores. Some universities will also consider the TOEFL (Test of English Foreign Language) exam, with a typical score of at least 101 overall with no section below 23. Again, it is worth checking with each university directly to ensure that they will consider TOEFL in place of IELTS, and to ensure that your score meets their specific criteria.

If you have not met the English language requirements prior to submitting your application, don't worry. Unless the university specifically states otherwise, the English language qualification score will be stipulated as part of a conditional offer.

Visas

International students will have to apply for a Tier 4 Student Visa before they are able to study in the UK. In order to get a Tier 4 Student Visa you will need a CAS (Confirmation of Acceptance for Studies) from the individual university which made the offer. In order to get a CAS, you will need to show various documents as set out by the admissions department. This can take time – there is no way of saying how much time as that will vary from country to country, but it can be days or weeks. The important thing is for you to apply for a CAS as soon as you are able.

As a consequence of Brexit, EU students will need to apply for a visa. EU residents who have already commenced their course prior to 1 January 2021 will not need to apply for a visa, but will need to apply for the EU Settlement Scheme in order to remain in the UK for the duration of their course.

The UCAS application form

Students who are studying outside the UK are often at a disadvantage because they may not have access to advisers who are familiar with the requirements of a successful UCAS application. The two areas that tend to be weakest are the personal statement and the reference.

Students who are unfamiliar with UCAS applications often write personal statements that concentrate too much on non-essential information (prizes, awards, responsibilities), and not enough on matters relevant to veterinary medicine. It might be useful to reflect on why you wish to study veterinary medicine in the UK rather than in your home country. Detailed advice on the personal statement can be found in Chapter 6 of this book. Similarly, your referee needs to be familiar with what the veterinary schools require in the reference; that is, your academic strengths and suitability for the course rather than merely a character reference. The UCAS website has a wealth of information, in relation to both personal statement and reference writing; particularly useful are the short videos that outline the key points about writing both of these documents. It is well worth ensuring that your chosen referee is familiar with this information before proceeding.

Work experience

Veterinary schools always require applicants to have gained some relevant work experience, even if you are classed as a non-standard applicant. Work experience tells the selectors that the candidates are serious about becoming vets and that they are familiar with what the profession demands. Gaining work experience can be difficult, but you should make every effort to do so. If it is impossible for you to gain veterinary work experience, you might try to substitute it with any work with animals, and by undertaking online placements or courses or by attending relevant lectures. It is important that the reference explains why there is no mention of work experience in the application, and what you did to try to get that experience.

Interviews

Most veterinary schools require students to attend interviews. This is often difficult to arrange for students who are not based in the UK. It is worth contacting the schools before you apply to see whether they are likely to require you to travel to the UK to be interviewed, though it is more likely that interviews will be conducted online, especially in the midst and the aftermath of the Covid-19 pandemic.

Studying outside the UK

An option for students who wish to study overseas, but want to undertake some of their clinical training in one of the UK veterinary schools, is the veterinary science course offered by St George's University in Grenada, West Indies. Another place that may be of interest is the Faculty of Medicine at Kosice, Slovak Republic, where the course is taught in English and accredited by the RCVS. For contact details for the course, see Chapter 12.

It is possible to practise as a vet in the UK having studied overseas; details are given on the RCVS website (www.rcvs.org.uk). You should ultimately check in advance though that your qualification will be accepted as a licence to practise veterinary medicine in Great Britain. The process is simpler for students who have studied in certain universities in Canada, Australia, South Africa or New Zealand where their degrees are approved by the RCVS. Further to the UK leaving the European Union, veterinary graduates from the EU need to closely follow emerging guidance from the RCVS.

Graduates from other countries can still practise in the UK if they pass the statutory examination for membership of the RCVS, which is held in a UK veterinary school in May/June each year. Further information for all overseas graduates can be obtained from www.rcvs.org.uk.

Mature students

A mature applicant is someone who is 21 years old or more on the first day of their studies.

In view of the extreme competition for places, it is unrealistic for mature students, at, say, 25 or 30 years of age, to expect special treatment. They should expect to satisfy the academic entry requirements in the usual way at one recent sitting and must have a good range of practical experience. However, this requirement has been known to be waived in exceptional cases, such as where a mature student displays strong motivation coupled with academic ability.

Mature applicants should use the personal statement section of the UCAS application to set out their qualifications and work experience. Your objective is to signal to the admissions tutors why they should see you. Your extra maturity and practical experience should show here. If you cannot get all the information in the space allowed, make sure you summarise what you want to get across in accordance with the bullet points in Chapter 6 (see pages 83–84) – why you want to study veterinary science, what you have done to explore this decision, how you respond to people, how you react under pressure, what your career aspirations are, and what your extracurricular interests are – in order to show that you are a rounded individual.

Remember, it is very important to show why you want to work with animals and to give details of any relevant work experience of a paid or voluntary nature. If you feel that the space in the personal statement section of the UCAS application does not permit you to do full justice to yourself, it is a good idea to prepare a CV or further documentation and send this directly to the veterinary school with your UCAS application number.

Students with disabilities and special educational needs

Students with disabilities and special educational needs are welcome at all institutions and are not disadvantaged. If you have a disability or health condition, you are encouraged to look at the demands of the course at the individual university. Those with a hearing or visual impairment are equally encouraged to apply. The institutions are fully committed to support students with additional needs, from dyslexia to physical disability, and have access arrangements in place. It is advisable in each situation to contact the universities individually and explain to them your circumstances as well as including details on the UCAS form. The more information you can give them, the better they will be able to advise you on what arrangements are in place. Provisions are usually made within the teaching facilities; some forms of accommodation may pose more of a logistical problem.

In terms of special educational needs, students who require a word processor or extra time will be allowed these in the same way that they would have been at school, subject to providing the correct documentation to the university.

For more information, refer directly to the university, which will probably have a person in charge of special access arrangements.

Fact: A cat can be either right-pawed or left-pawed.

9 | A bird in the hand
Results day

The A level results will arrive at your school on the third Thursday in August typically (though this may differ in 2021 as a consequence of the pandemic). For International Baccalaureate (IB) qualifications results day will be in the first week of July and for students studying in Scotland it will be the first week of August. The veterinary schools will have received them a few days earlier. You must make sure that you are at home on the day the results are published and able to travel in to your school or college to collect them. If you are unable to do this, speak to your school or college about making arrangements for your results to be given to you by phone or email as early as possible on the day; don't wait for the school to post the results slip to you. If you need to act to secure a place, you may have to do so quickly. This chapter will take you through the steps you should take after receiving your results and also explains what to do if your grades are below what you expected.

If things go wrong during the exams

If something happens when you are preparing for or actually taking the exams that prevents you from doing your best, you must notify your school/college, the exam board and the veterinary schools that have made you offers. This notification will come best from your head teacher and should include your UCAS number and date of birth. Send it off at once; it is no good waiting for disappointing results and then telling everyone that you felt ghastly at the time but said nothing to anyone. Exam boards can give you special consideration if the appropriate forms are sent to them by the school, along with supporting evidence. An increasing number of veterinary schools now only accept mitigating circumstances if they were reported to the exam board at the time of the examination.

Your extenuating circumstances must be significant. A 'slight sniffle' won't do! If you really are sufficiently ill to be unable to prepare for the exams or to perform effectively during them, you must consult your GP and obtain a letter describing your condition.

The other main cause of underperformance is distressing events at home. If a member of your immediate family is very seriously ill, or if you have some form of significant domestic upheaval, you should explain this to your head teacher and ask them to write to the examiners and veterinary schools.

With luck, the exam board will give you the benefit of the doubt if your marks fall on a grade boundary. Equally, you can hope that the veterinary school will allow you to slip one grade below the conditional offer, although this is rare now that there are so many applicants chasing a small number of places. If things work out badly, then the fact that you declared extenuating circumstances should ensure that you are treated sympathetically if you decide to reapply through UCAS.

The veterinary school admissions departments are well organised and efficient, but they are staffed by human beings. If there were extenuating circumstances that could have affected your exam performance and that were brought to their notice in June, it is a good idea to ask them to review the relevant letters shortly before the exam results are published.

If you hold an offer and get the grades

If you previously received a conditional offer and your grades equal or exceed that offer, congratulations! You can relax and wait for your chosen medical school to send you joining instructions. One word of warning: you cannot assume that grades of A*AB satisfy an AAA offer. This is especially true if the B grade is in biology or chemistry. You should call your chosen university as soon as possible to check if you have met your offer.

If you have good grades but no offer

Very few schools keep places open and, of those that do, most will choose to allow applicants who hold a conditional offer to slip a grade rather than dust off a reserve list of those they interviewed but didn't make an offer to. They are even less likely to consider applicants who appear out of the blue, no matter how high their grades are. In recent years, a small number of universities have offered Clearing places. With the increased number of places being made available for studying veterinary medicine at university, it is possible that more spaces will be available through Clearing, although this is not an option that should be relied on.

If you hold three A grades but were rejected when you applied through UCAS, you need to let the veterinary schools know that you are out there. The best way to do this is by phone and email. Places available to students in this position are few and far between, so it is preferable to phone in order to make contact as quickly as possible. Contact details are listed in the UCAS directory and are on the university websites.

With most competitive courses, a few places will be available, and the most proactive students who are quick off the mark on results day are most likely to secure an interview. If you find yourself in this situation, be prepared to interview at short notice!

The most likely scenario is that you will have to reapply through UCAS in the next admissions cycle. Although you will already have the grades for entry in this situation, it is important to understand that there are a number of other elements of your application that you'll need to work on to maximise your chances of securing a place. Things to consider are listed below.

- Your personal statement – revisit it and cast a critical eye over it. This is also an opportunity to add in any work placements or other positive experiences that you have had since your last application.
- Your work experience – any opportunity to add further work experience to your profile will always be a good step. Whether it is veterinary-related or just general voluntary work, it will have a positive impact.

UCAS Adjustment

There is a system called UCAS Adjustment that allows applicants who pass their exams with better results than expected to get a place at a higher-level university. However, this is not likely to be the case for veterinary school as they all require high grades and you would not have been made an offer that required lower grades. You can enter Adjustment only if your results have met and exceeded the conditions of your conditional firm choice. A student must have held a conditional firm choice on their application to be eligible, and so, if you have had no offers, it is not something you can use. In short, Adjustment doesn't help if you have applied to veterinary schools.

If you hold an offer but miss the grades

If you have only narrowly missed the required grades, it is important that you contact the admissions team as soon as possible. As mentioned previously, you will probably know what their decision is at this point, thanks to the UCAS website. If you have been rejected, it is vital that you keep a level head and do not panic; you must stay calm throughout. If you have not been rejected outright or are unsure of their decision, you must contact the admissions team by telephone – so ensure that in the run-up to results day you have gathered together the contact numbers of the universities you have accepted as your firm and insurance choices.

In some cases, veterinary schools will allow applicants who hold a conditional offer to slip a grade (particularly if they came across well at the interview stage) rather than offering the place to somebody else. However, be warned – this is a rare occurrence and most of the time dropping a grade will result in outright rejection.

When speaking to the universities, they are likely to give you a simple yes or no answer or tell you that you are still being considered. It is unlikely that crying, begging or pleading your case to the person on the phone will make any difference to the overall decision. If they tell you that you have been rejected, there are some questions you should ask.

- Would they consider your application if you applied next year (i.e. do they accept resit students)?
- What would the likely grade requirements be? (They will almost certainly ask for at least AAA, but it is worth checking anyway.)
- Would they interview you again?

If at all possible, get something in writing to refer to when reapplying.

In some rare cases, veterinary schools may hold your offer for the following year, allowing you to resit your exams and achieve the grades second time around, though this should not be relied upon.

Retaking A levels

Many unsuccessful candidates decide to do a repeat year and take their examinations again. Before doing this it would be sensible to seek the advice of an admissions tutor. The fact is that not many people doing repeats are made unconditional offers unless there are documented extenuating circumstances, such as serious illness. If you are made an offer it will usually be based upon the second attempt and the requirement could be raised to achieving one grade higher than the published offer across the three subjects. You may get a repeat offer if you have narrowly failed to secure a place on the first try and are excellent in all other respects.

The truth is that the almost overwhelming pressure of demand from highly motivated and well-qualified candidates is taking its toll on the chances of those repeating A levels. Selection is becoming more stringent, resulting in fewer resitters being successful. However, you are still encouraged to do so.

Retakes are considered by universities depending on the specific policy of the institution you are applying to. In most cases the policy is that students can retake without penalty; however, you must achieve the offer grades in the second sitting. Most universities say that you must complete the qualification within two years and one resit is allowed, though if this takes place in a third year, the entry requirement will increase.

Reapplying

In order to reapply, you have to go through exactly the same process again, taking into account all that has been said above. However, when reapplying, make sure you update your application. A careless application would be one that does not include anything new about what you have planned – and worse, it does not update a personal statement!

Make sure that you talk to admissions tutors about your chances before you reapply, as they will be able to advise on whether your application would be considered. It is important to research this carefully to ensure that you do not waste one of your four options on a university that will not be able to consider you.

If you had extenuating circumstances first time round, then mention them at this point but make sure they are compelling – not just 'I had a cold on the day'!

If this round of applications is not fruitful, then fear not. Applying once you have your resit grades in hand can often lead to more success with applications, providing the rest of your application is strong; you will be viewed as less of a risk by veterinary schools who will be able to make you an unconditional offer.

Fact: Chocolate is poisonous to both cats and dogs. Surprisingly though, it is the most effective type of mice bait – mice don't really like cheese that much at all!

10 | Counting sheep
Financing your course

Whether undertaking an undergraduate or postgraduate course, the cost of studying is considerable. This has been exacerbated in recent years by rises in living costs and the large increases in university tuition fees in 2010. In 2020, the UK Parliament's House of Commons Library released student loan statistics that revealed that, on average, students graduating in 2019 had a debt of £40,000. NB, these figures are based on an average of *all* students, rather than focusing on veterinary students. As well as veterinary medicine courses being longer in duration, veterinary students have additional course-related expenses, such as travel expenses, placement fees, appropriate clothing, equipment and books. While many students might make the most of their holidays to work and earn additional money, veterinary students will have to spend most of their time on EMR/EMS placements in order to meet the prescribed experience required for their training.

On the whole, the cost of studying will fluctuate depending on:

- geographical location: living in London will be more expensive than living in other cities in the UK
- area of permanent residence: there are differences in fees payable and the financial support available depending on your nationality
- family support: contributions from family members may significantly help reduce the costs accrued
- availability of scholarships: some universities provide financial support for students meeting particular criteria, such as academic excellence
- part-time work: this is difficult to manage while studying any course, but especially veterinary medicine, yet working while studying could help to reduce the overall burden of debt.

When considering levels of student debt, it is easy to become disheartened and think that university study is not for you. What all students must remember is that tuition fees do not have to be paid up front; in fact, most students receive student loans to cover this cost. In addition, the loans do not start to be paid back until you are earning over a certain amount. The full details of this will be discussed later in the chapter.

Regardless of how much debt you incur, or how you fund your way through university, hopefully the figures discussed below will help you to realise that undertaking a course such as veterinary medicine should only be done after seriously considering the overall cost and carefully examining your ability to be fully committed to your study for the full five years.

To find out what the fees are and what funding is available for veterinary medicine courses, you should explore each of the universities' websites and talk to their financial departments, because fees and funding procedures vary from university to university.

Fees

UK students

Students who are UK nationals pay lower tuition fees than both EU and non-EU international students. For 2021 entry, universities will continue to charge up to £9,250 per year for tuition fees; it is expected that this figure will continue to rise in the future in line with inflation. Fees are charged in line with the government's Teaching Excellence Framework (TEF), which assesses universities and colleges on the quality of their teaching. The institutions with a TEF award are able to charge £9,250, whereas those without a TEF award are only able to charge £9,000.

There are a number of differences between the systems in England, Scotland, Wales and Northern Ireland. From September 2018, the rules were as follows, although they may be subject to change in the future.

- Students living in England are liable for full fees across the UK except for at Welsh universities, where the maximum amount charged is £9,000 per academic year.
- Students living in Scotland who study full time at a Scottish university do not pay tuition fees as long as eligibility criteria are met. Scottish students are required to pay fees of up to £9,250 per academic year in England or Northern Ireland and £9,000 in Wales.
- For students residing in Wales, up to £9,250 per academic year will be payable if studying at an English, Scottish or Northern Irish university. Welsh students wanting to study in Wales have their fees subsidised by the Welsh Assembly and so are only required to pay up to £4,046 per year.
- Students living in Northern Ireland who wish to study in Northern Ireland will pay £4,365 per academic year; to study elsewhere in the UK they are required to pay up to £9,250 per academic year in England or Scotland and £9,000 in Wales.

EU and non-EU international students

In an announcement in June 2020, the Universities Minister in the UK, Michelle Donelan, stated that from August 2021, EU, other EEA and

Swiss nationals will no longer qualify for home fee status for degree level study, and they will no longer be able to access financial support from Student Finance England. Instead, universities will set their own fees for EU students, with many of these yet to be finalised but with a view that they are likely to be in line with fees for non-EU international students. The RVC, for example, will charge both EU and non-EU international students £36,760 per year from 2021. The respective governments in Northern Ireland, Wales and Scotland later confirmed that the same changes to EU fee status would be applied as in England from 2021.

For international students, the costs of studying in the UK are significantly greater and can often be prohibitive. In line with the RVC's tuition fees outlined above, the University of Edinburgh's fees are £34,550 per academic year for overseas students. While there is some variation in cost between universities, these fees are broadly representative of the whole of the UK.

Table 4 Annual tuition fees by region for courses starting in 2021

Student's home region	Studying in England	Studying in Scotland	Studying in Wales	Studying in Northern Ireland
England	Up to £9,250	Up to £9,250	Up to £9,000	Up to £9,250
Scotland	Up to £9,250	No fee	Up to £9,000	Up to £9,250
Wales	Up to £9,250	Up to £9,250	Up to £4,046	Up to £9,250
Northern Ireland	Up to £9,250	Up to £9,250	Up to £9,000	Up to £4,395
EU & other international	Variable	Variable	Variable	Variable

Source: www.ucas.com/ucas/undergraduate/finance-and-support.

Funding

There are a number of sources of financial help that are potentially available for full-time students from the UK to help cover the cost of university study. The main ones are student loans and bursaries, which are allocated according to individual and family circumstances. It is important to apply as soon as possible through the Student Finance online service in order to prevent delay in receiving this assistance. There are different student finance sites to use depending on which country you are a permanent resident of. These sites contain detailed information on the help that is available and how to apply for it:

- England: Student Finance – www.gov.uk/studentfinance
- Scotland: Student Awards Agency for Scotland (SAAS) – www. saas.gov.uk

- Wales: Student Finance Wales – www.studentfinancewales.co.uk
- Northern Ireland: Student Finance Northern Ireland – www.student financeni.co.uk

For the most recent figures, please check the relevant student finance websites regularly.

Student loans

The most common way for students to finance their studies is by taking out a student loan. If you are an eligible, full-time student, you can take out two types of loan: a loan for tuition fees and a maintenance loan to meet living costs. The tuition fees loan does not depend on your household income and is paid straight to the university to cover the full cost. You can borrow all or part of the amount required to cover your fees.

The amount of maintenance loan you are entitled to depends on several factors, including household income, where you live while you're studying and what year of study you are in. For example, if you're living away from home, the maximum maintenance loan for English students is £9,203 for the academic year 2020–21, although if you're studying in London the maximum loan is £12,010. The maximum available is less if you're living with your parents during term time. The details are shown in Table 5 below.

It is vital to remember when considering student loans that both the tuition fee and living expenses loans are not like loans you would get from a bank as you only start paying it back when you have a job that pays over a certain amount. Currently these thresholds are £26,575 per annum (before deductions) for English and Welsh students and £19,390 for Scottish and Northern Irish students. The repayments are then taken directly from your pay packet by your employer.

Table 5 Maximum maintenance loans available in 2021

Term-time living arrangements	England	Scotland	Wales	Northern Ireland
Living at home	£7,747	£7,750	£1,450	£5,338
Living away from home, outside of London	£9,203	£7,750	£1,710	£6,428
Living away from home, in London	£12,010	£7,750	£2,136	Up to £9,250

Source: www.gov.uk/student-finance/new-fulltime-students. Contains public sector information licensed under the Open Government Licence.

Grants

Historically, the maintenance grant was available to help students with accommodation and other living costs and did not have to be repaid. However, in September 2016, the maintenance grant system was abolished for English students, and as a result, any funding received is now in the form of a loan. Means-tested grants for Scottish, Northern Irish and Welsh students still exist, although this situation may change in the future. If your application for a maintenance grant is successful, the value of this will be deducted from your maintenance loan. The details of grants available are listed below for each country:

England

Most grants have been abolished. Some support may be available to certain students, e.g. students with children and students with a disability.

Scotland

Students under the age of 25 may be entitled to the Young Students Bursary (YSB), which is the equivalent of a grant. Currently, if your household income is under £21,000, you receive a maximum of £2,000. This amount then tapers to zero if you have a household income of £34,000 or more per annum. Support may also be available to certain students, for example, lone parents and students with a disability.

Wales

The Welsh Government Learning Grant (WGLG) is a grant available depending on household income. Currently, if household income is less than £18,370 per annum, the maximum amount of £8,100 is payable if you are living away from home. This reduces on a sliding scale to a minimum of £1,000 if income exceeds £59,200 per annum. Up to £6,885 is accessible for those who stay at home while studying, while £10,214 is available to those students studying in London.

Additionally, a Special Support Grant (SSG) is available for certain individuals depending on circumstances. For example, this can be paid if you are a single parent, have a disability or are in receipt of certain benefits. For the academic year 2020–21, the maximum is £12,260 for those studying in London, £9,810 for those studying outside of London and £8,335 for those staying at home.

Northern Ireland

Special Support Grants or Maintenance Grants are available in part if household income is less than £41,065. The full grant of £3,475 is awarded if household income is £19,203 or less, and this tapers to zero up to an income of £41,065. Additional support is available to certain students, for example, lone parents and students with a disability.

Scholarships and bursaries

The veterinary schools offer scholarships and bursaries and further advice on sources of funding. There are also general bursaries and scholarships, some of which are specifically for veterinary medicine students. You should read the websites of the universities in order to find out whether you will be able to get a reduction in fees. These are variable between veterinary schools and even within veterinary schools year on year, so careful research into these options is required. For scholarships, further information can be found at www. thescholarshiphub.org.uk.

Armed Forces bursaries are grants to selected veterinary students who pass their Army Officer Selection Board examinations for both professionally qualified officers and for the Royal Army Veterinary Corps, and who apply before their second year of university. You must begin initial Officer training before your 29th birthday. In return, you have to spend four years in the service. For more details, see https://apply.army.mod. uk/roles/army-medical-service/veterinary-officer.

Keeping costs down: hints and tips

- Avoid buying lots of kit or textbooks in advance. When you get to the course you may find some discounts are offered. Second-hand textbooks may be for sale from former veterinary students.
- Check for student travel concessions and get advice on the best offers on the regular trips that you will have to make.
- Apply early for the student loan, as it takes some time for the loan to be processed.
- Set yourself a limit on how much you are prepared to spend each term. Remember: the more partying, the worse your bank account will look.
- Easter is a time when it is possible for students to augment their income. Once you have gained experience with your first lambing, students say that it is possible, if you are lucky, to make over £300 per week. This is very hard work, involving 12-hour days, seven days a week, for a minimum of three weeks. But it will certainly improve your bank account – and give you valuable experience.

Expected student expenditure

The following two lists show the estimated additional course costs (2020/21) for students applying to veterinary science courses at the University of Cambridge.

Veterinary Medicine (pre-clinical)

Lab coat	£9.96
Overalls (boiler suit)	£16.54
Waterproof trousers	£7.97
Dissection kit, gloves, safety glasses, loan of locker and key, loan of dog skeleton	£24.00
Veterinary Dissection Manual, which includes course guides for Veterinary Anatomy and Physiology (1st Year) and Neurobiology and Comparative Veterinary Biology (2nd Year)	£14.00
Wellington boots	£6.95
University-approved calculator	£20.00
Electron micrographs (optional)	£2.00
EMS (pre-clinical) 12 weeks' practical vacation experience with animals, particularly farm animals. Insurance cover provided but no subsistence grants payable	Variable

Veterinary medicine (clinical)

Locker padlock	£7.50
Clinical thermometer	£4.03
Digital thermometer	£5.40
6" scissors curved on flat	£2.90
Spencer Wells forceps 5"	£3.84
Pen torch	£1.44
Dog lead (red)	£1.26
Hoof pick	£0.69
Nail clippers, stainless steel	£10.00 approx.
Yard boots	Self-purchase
Stethoscope (this is a basic level stethoscope; many students purchase a higher quality stethoscope later in the clinical course)	£2.82
EMS – 26 weeks required by RCVS (grants are available to assist with costs)	Variable depending on chosen placements
BVA insurance cover for 4th-, 5th- and 6th-year students	£42.00 – met by veterinary school
White theatre shoes (Year 6)	£22.68 approx.
Protective clothing for theatre (Year 6)	£6.18 approx.

Case study

Jade studied at the University of Surrey. She did well in her A levels but was unsure of what she wanted to study at university, so took a year out before eventually deciding to go down the route of veterinary medicine.

'I finished sixth form with good grades in English, History and Politics but I had no idea what to do at uni so I went straight into work. During my year out I managed to secure not only a retail job but also voluntary experience at a local animal shelter and it was then that I realised that I really wanted to be a vet. It had been a dream of mine as a child that I thought I'd grown out of, but apparently not!'

Jade spent three months volunteering in the kennels before eventually also taking up animal fostering.

'It was my love of animals that initially drew me in and ultimately became the decisive factor in my choice of degree. Unfortunately I didn't have A levels in any sciences so I took intensive courses in biology and chemistry (gaining As in both) before I then applied to Surrey to study veterinary medicine and science. It wasn't the most straightforward of routes but I'm glad things went the way that they did. I'm also really pleased that I took the time out to work and volunteer because I was able to really think about what course I wanted to do and do my research rather than rush into three or more years of study in something I wasn't really passionate about.

'My course was amazing, but definitely hard work, too. I did two weeks of calving during my first Easter break, which was a great experience. I was really nervous going into it as I had heard that most farmers don't think women are capable of working with large animals but that wasn't my experience at all. The farmers were all incredibly helpful and let me get really stuck in.'

Fact: A puppy is born blind, deaf and toothless.

11| Snakes and ladders
Career paths

There may be hidden expenses in training to be a vet, but at least you can reflect, with some optimism, that a degree in veterinary science is going to result in a professional qualification and a job. According to figures published in the RCVS's annual RCVS Facts report for 2018 (the last published date), over 85% of registered surgeons were in practice and roughly 76% of those were in the UK.

The BVA has warned that following Brexit, urgent work will be required to safeguard against the anticipated shortfall of veterinary surgeons working in the UK. As such, there may be an increased call for qualified veterinarians in the years that follow to ensure that veterinary coverage is sufficient across the UK.

Professional Development Phase

Once you have graduated from your veterinary degree course, you are still not there yet. The year after graduation is known as the Professional Development Phase (PDP), during which you will be expected to develop your skills. The RCVS has developed a set of Competences so that you can record your progress. After that you will always be expected to keep up with your CPD by attending courses and lectures and networking.

Once you have qualified, you might wish to consider working in the types of practice or roles described in this chapter.

Career opportunities

The universities' first-destination statistics show that nearly all veterinary graduates begin their careers in practice, but such is the variety of opportunity in this profession that career change and divergence can and do occur. For example, graduates are employed in government service dealing with investigation, control and eradication of diseases. There are also opportunities for veterinary scientists to become engaged in university teaching and research establishments at home and abroad.

If you start in general practice, there is the chance to move into different types of practice. The trend is towards small-animal practices, but there is also more opportunity to work with horses – now seen as an important part of the growing leisure industry. There is also a growing trend towards specialisation within practices. Areas of specialisation include cattle, horses, household pets and even exotics. Specialisation can also be more sophisticated – for example, combining equine care with lameness in all animals. Dermatology, soft tissues and cardiology are examples of the kinds of specialisation that are seen as helpful to clients. It is possible for postgraduate specialist qualifications to be obtained through the RCVS's specialist certificate and diploma examinations.

Postgraduate courses

Education in the field of veterinary medicine is continuous; not only that, as a profession, it places a high emphasis on CPD. It is incredibly important to keep yourself up to date and also educate yourself on the variety of different jobs available to you, as the degree course itself – while comprehensive – is not exhaustive, as it cannot be. There are both full-time and part-time postgraduate courses, and they can focus on anything from the welfare of animals to infectious diseases to education. These programmes are designed for anyone looking to advance their knowledge of a specialist part of the profession through research. The postgraduate courses are not restricted to the eight veterinary schools but are available in a range of universities; you can take postgraduate courses in anything from Animal Behaviour at Newcastle University to Aquatic Veterinary Studies at the University of Stirling. Courses vary in length depending on whether you are doing the self-study option or a taught one-year course. It is a big factor to consider, i.e. whether you can take a full year off financially or, as with most professionals, to study alongside working.

It is important to note that you do not need a postgraduate course in order to get employment in the profession. These courses are for those who wish to specialise or move into a niche field, such as aquatic veterinary medicine.

These courses have their obvious benefits, i.e. they will allow you to specialise in specific areas of the profession. It is often advised, though, that you spend some time working as a professional first after your clinical years. It is wise to take a step back and assess your options once you have completed training before making any decisions on your career course.

Veterinary variety: types of vet

With more registered vets than in recent years and an increase in the number of new registrations, the veterinary field still has its problems as a result of the recession. Pet owners are feeling the pinch, which in turn impacts on vets. Smaller vet practices are facing competition from big corporations with marketing budgets, making it harder for them to compete. As your degree progresses, you will most likely find an area of veterinary medicine that you particularly enjoy or have a certain flair for. Before you reach that stage, though, it is worthwhile considering which area immediately strikes you as something to which you feel you could dedicate the next 40 years of your working life.

However, it is highly advisable to start your career in general practice, working with household animals or even with larger animals on a farm, before perhaps opting to specialise in one of the more diverse forms of veterinary surgery.

Small-animal vet

The last RCVS survey in 2019 revealed that about 53% of qualified vets working in the profession work mainly or entirely in small-animal practice, which has jumped considerably from 2010 when the figure was 46%. This vet works in local practice dealing with the care and treatment of household pets. You will be concerned with anything from vaccinations to neutering, as well as local surgery and general health check-ups. In unfortunate situations, you may be required to make the decision as to the kindness of putting an animal down to end its pain.

Large-animal vet

Principally concerned with multiple animals in a group as opposed to individual animals, a large-animal vet is most often found on a farm, and is concerned with the health and productivity of the herd. Your responsibilities are likely to involve the treatment of disease and giving advice on the husbandry of the animals, including nutritional balance and sanitation. This role requires a strong will and a thick skin when dealing with farmers, who are an entirely different clientele to the ordinary public as their animals are livestock reared for profit rather than kept as pets.

Equine vet

As the name suggests, equine vets specialise in the treatment of horses. Stable and horse owners alike prefer to use a specialist equine vet when it comes to the treatment of their animals because horses are different from other animals in all respects – from anatomy to pharmacology.

Horses also require different husbandry and, therefore, as a specialist you will be giving a different form of advice. Before specialising in this area, it is essential, or at least highly advisable, that you gain experience in general practice and then progress to achieving your specialist qualifications later on, once you have general experience to your name.

Exotic-animal vet

Exotic-animal vets have specialist training in the treatment of exotic animals including snakes and turtles. The term 'exotic' is wide ranging, and it is worth remembering that ferrets and small rodents are included in this category. As with an equine vet, becoming a general vet first is a prerequisite to taking your specialist qualifications. There is an element of glamour in this work and you can expect to find yourself spending a lot of time at a zoo working with wild animals.

A rise in the number of exotic animals being kept as pets has meant that there is a new angle being promoted within vet student training. The Hospital for Small Animals at The Royal (Dick) School in Edinburgh has led the way by opening a specialist exotic unit for veterinary student training.

Avian vet

Avian vets are concerned with the treatment of birds, and this specialisation offers you a varied working environment. One day might be spent in private practice, the next in a bird sanctuary and the next in a zoo. You would certainly never be bored! However, you should take prior work in general small-animal practice before specialising with the requisite qualifications, as working with smaller animals will help you appreciate the smaller anatomical size of a bird.

Advice: Usually you need to have a couple of years post-graduation experience before you can – or should – start a qualification to specialise in exotic or avian veterinary medicine.

Other types of vet

The vets listed above are the most common types of veterinary surgeons in the UK. However, this list is by no means comprehensive and, should you wish to, you can also specialise in the following areas:

- Anaesthesia and analgesia
- Animal welfare, ethics and law
- Behavioural medicine
- Camelid health and production
- Cardiology

- Cattle health and production (general, dairy or mastitis)
- Dentistry (including further specialisation into equine dentistry)
- Dermatology
- Diagnostic imaging (large animal)
- Emergency and critical care
- Endocrinology (small animal)
- Epidemiology
- Feline medicine
- Fish health and reproduction
- Gastroenterology (small animal)
- Internal medicine (equine or small animal)
- Neurology (including further specialisation for small animal)
- Nutrition (or clinical nutrition with further specialisation for equine)
- Oncology (general, small animal or surgical/surgical small animal, radiation)
- Ophthalmology
- Orthopaedics (small animal, surgery – small animal or surgery – equine)
- Parasitology
- Pathology (general or clinical; equine, farm animals, microbiology, small domestic animal, laboratory animals or zoo and wildlife)
- Pharmacology and toxicology
- Pig medicine
- Poultry medicine and production
- Public health
- Reproduction (general, cattle and sheep, equine or theriogenology)
- Sheep health and reproduction
- Small animal medicine
- Soft tissue surgery (equine or small animal)
- Sports medicine (equine)
- Surgery (equine or small animal)
- Wildlife medicine (mammalian)
- Zoo and wildlife medicine (general, avian, mammal, small mammal, wildlife population health or zoo health management).

The veterinary practice

There are many different types of veterinary practice. The majority, however, deal with all species. Others tend to specify the size of the animal, i.e. some deal solely with large animals, some small, and others only equine. The size of practices varies a great deal. The average size is three or four vets working together, but a few are smaller or much larger. Some are incredibly busy, while others may manage to convey an easier atmosphere while being equally hard-working. Some practices offer particular facilities which define them as different types of veterinary practice.

The structure of a general practice

In a general practice, a veterinary surgeon is responsible for all types of treatment, from medical to surgical, of all animals. It is not uncommon for veterinary surgeons to study for further qualifications offered by the RCVS while working in order to further their knowledge about certain animals. Veterinary surgeons are vital to the practice and most start as a locum or an associate. Most practices are partnerships run by several veterinary surgeons with one principal. The goal of most associates working in a practice is to reach partnership level. This then involves separate business skills in order to ensure that the practice is making money.

The principal, or practice manager, is usually found in a larger practice as it is important to have one person who has a general overview of the business. This person will be responsible for ensuring that all monies are paid and that the practice is run to a high standard. This role is not common to all practices, as many cannot afford an extra level of support.

From a veterinary surgeon's point of view, the most important people within the practice are veterinary nurses. They ensure that standards of care are high and that both animals and owners are kept comfortable. They assist in supportive care, and also undertake minor surgical procedures and tests, should they be required.

The receptionists are the first point of contact within a practice. A lot of owners will be very disturbed when bringing their animal to the vet and it is the receptionist's responsibility to present a calm and professional approach that will reassure the clients. They are also gatekeepers and personal assistants for the veterinary surgeons, making sure that appointments are managed and schedules are adhered to.

Veterinary practice as a small business

A veterinary practice is dependent upon the income it makes, which is generated by the surgery itself, in order to be a successful small business. It does not receive money from an external source, such as the government. The practice's income is used to pay the staff and the rent (if the site is not owned by the practice) and then the rest is put back into the business to pay for equipment and up-to-date technology.

Vets are often faced with a moral dilemma when seeing a client who cannot afford to pay the veterinary fees for their services. Fees can often be very high and many clients (who are used to human healthcare often being free of charge) are shocked by what they are required to pay for the treatment of their pets. Vets need to be understanding in this sort of situation, but it's important to remember that you are part of a business and this is your livelihood.

Accreditation

All practices need to adhere to the codes of practice of a specific regulatory body.

RCVS accredited practice

The RCVS Practice Standards Scheme was launched on 1 January 2005. It is the only scheme representing the veterinary profession and is a regulatory body set up to ensure the highest standards. If you were to work in an RCVS-accredited practice, you would be dedicated to maintaining the highest possible standard of veterinary care; to providing a greater amount of information regarding the care of animals to the public and to clients; and to being at the cutting edge of advancements within the field of veterinary science.

BEVA listed practice

The British Equine Veterinary Association (BEVA) has compiled a list of self-certified practices in the equine industry and has a code of practice for veterinary surgeons in this field.

AVMA accredited course

The American Veterinary Medical Association is the North American accrediting council for veterinary surgeons. However, in order to practise medicine in North America, students must pass the North American Veterinary Licensing Examination (NAVLE).

EAEVE

The European Association of Establishments for Veterinary Education (EAEVE) currently provides assurance of the veterinary degree in Europe and its standards; the RVC and universities of Copenhagen, Helsinki and Zurich/Bern are the only establishments that currently hold full accreditation.

Government service

In the public sector, vets are involved in protecting public health, working in government departments and agencies such as the Animal Health and Veterinary Laboratories Agency (AHVLA), the Food Standards Agency and the Veterinary Medicines Directorate. Defra employs vets to monitor animal health and to prevent the spread of diseases.

Most of the veterinary surgeons employed by Defra work in the AHVLA. Field officers have a wide range of responsibilities, which include the control of major epidemic diseases of farm animals, matters of consumer protection (largely in relation to meat hygiene), the control of import and export of animals and the operation of health schemes.

The AHVLA comprises officers who are based in laboratories. Their job is to operate and support control schemes in the interests of public health, to monitor developments and give early warning of any disease problems or dangers to the safety of the food chain. They also provide practising vets with a chargeable diagnostic service. The Veterinary Laboratories Agency (VLA), which has now merged with the AHVLA at Weybridge in Surrey, employs veterinary surgeons who carry out research and provide support for various field activities.

The Veterinary Medicines Directorate deals with the licensing of drugs.

Veterinary teaching and research

Veterinary researchers play a vital role in advancing our understanding of diseases. Research in this field enhances the health, welfare and usefulness of both food-producing and companion animals, and helps to safeguard the public from diseases. Investigations of a comparative nature also help us to understand and manage human disease, for example in cancer, genetics, reproduction and infections. The majority of research takes place at the university veterinary schools and at research institutes (which, unlike veterinary practices, are financed by the government), in laboratories and in private enterprise. Many careers in research span the interface between human and veterinary medicine, which provides a huge scope for variety in the role.

A qualification in veterinary science is more than a licence to practise. It can also open up opportunities for those interested in university teaching and research at home and overseas. In addition to clinical research work, some veterinary surgeons undergo further postgraduate training in the biological sciences. Specialisation is possible in physiology, pathology, microbiology, nutrition, genetics and statistics. Veterinary scientists are not exclusively found working in institutions concerned with animal health and disease; they can also work in natural science laboratories, medical schools and medical research institutes. The opportunities are there for young veterinary surgeons attracted by a research career.

Veterinary schools provide some of the referral hospitals to which veterinary surgeons can refer cases needing more specialised treatment. For example, recent success in the treatment of equine colic stemmed from early recognition and referral of appropriate cases allied to developments in anaesthesia and monitoring, improved surgical techniques and suture materials, plus better post-operative care. Good teamwork between the referring practitioner and the university specialists plays a big part.

Veterinary graduates are employed as research scientists by Defra, the Biotechnology and Biological Sciences Research Council, the Animal Health Trust, and in pharmaceutical and other industrial research organisations.

Case study

Mary Cecilia graduated from Nottingham University in 2012. She has been working in a veterinary surgery in Suffolk ever since.

'An office job was never for me, neither my mother nor my father were in one so it never struck me as something I was keen to join. I have been working as a vet now for little over four years since graduating. Would I say it has been rewarding? Absolutely yes. Would I say it had been easy? Are you kidding me?! No, but that is what makes the job so fulfilling, every day is different and forces me to keep learning, to adapt, to discover. I am so grateful that I am in a job that offers lifelong learning.

'One of the most gratifying things is the love that the animals give you. Think of the feeling you get from your pet and it is that but with a variety of animals on a daily cycle. Not all the animals are friendly though; what is important is that you remember that they are coming to see you because there is something wrong with them, they cannot communicate that with you, therefore you need to understand that it is not personal. It certainly is not that.

'The investigative side of the job is the bit I am drawn to most. The process, the interpretation of the data, the administration of treatment, it really does enable mental stimulation. I always found the mathematics side hard though, so calculating drug dosage or similar is a little more mental stimulation that I can take at times!

'Surgery is the biggest challenge from a skills point of view. It is a very daunting feeling knowing that you hold the life of the animal in your hands, though only if you stop and think about it, which, to be brutally honest, with a trainee vet, you don't once you have done your first few surgeries. It is an integral part of the job and you would be amazed how quickly any nervousness is overridden by sharp and complete focus. Myself, I like to play classical music while concentrating, I have always believed in the studies that show that it increases alertness. I know others do it differently and I have many colleagues who have their own process.

"he hardest part of the job is the part you wish you never had to do; putting an animal to sleep. I won't dwell on this, other than to say, steel yourself as early as you can. No one says don't be empathetic, if anything it will make you a better vet if you are; the point is to separate human feeling from what is in the best interest of the animal. That is challenge number one. Challenge number two is to deal with the pet owner. My only advice is compassion is a compelling argument if an animal is suffering.

'So, I heartily promote and champion the veterinary profession. I don't think it is without its faults, or its hardships, as most professions are; however, what I do think is that it is the most wonderfully diverse, gratifying process you can be part of and, as with anything, what you get out of it will be defined by what you put in. Be robust: remember there will be difficult customers. Be resilient: for there will be hard times. Be ruthless (not quite): because you are running a business at the end of the day and keeping a pet is expensive. Be rewarded: daily, by not forgetting the privileged role you are in, one where you get to help animals and people and to go to work every day doing what you most enjoy.'

Other career paths

The Army employs veterinary scientists in the Royal Army Veterinary Corps, where they care for service animals, mostly working dogs and horses used for ceremonial purposes. They also have public health responsibilities and opportunities for research or postgraduate study. Those recruited join with the rank of an Army captain for a four-year Short Service Commission, but this may be altered to a Regular Commission on application.

Some veterinary surgeons prefer to work for animal welfare societies, such as the RSPCA, PDSA and Blue Cross. Others work as inspectors for the Home Office.

Average salaries

When considering the salaries for qualified veterinarians, there is a great deal of variation based on the level of experience, type of practice and level of specialisation. Table 6 (opposite) summarises the average salaries of vets working within the UK at various stages in their career.

Table 6 Expected annual earnings, pre bonus, add-ons and profit share (approx. and variable) – Veterinary Surgeon

Salary	Level
£29,421	Early career
£39,062	Mid career
£43,656	Experienced
£43,989	>21 years

Source: www.payscale.com/research/UK/Job=Veterinarian/Salary
Reprinted with kind permission from www.payscale.com

Veterinary nurses

Veterinary nurses work alongside veterinary surgeons and provide full support in veterinary surgeries or hospitals, ensuring the highest standard of care for the animals. Their work covers a wide range of duties, such as diagnostic tests, treatments and minor surgery; they also are involved in major surgery, monitoring the animals while under anaesthetic. One crucial role of a veterinary nurse is education – teaching owners about animal husbandry. Veterinary nurses have good opportunities for career advancement and the longer they have worked in a particular practice, the more responsibility they will be given, for example managerial tasks such as managing teams either in a surgery or in an animal hospital. They will also be required to train new members of staff.

There are opportunities available in different environments too, such as veterinary research, universities, kennels and zoos, which can be alternative career paths for anyone unable to obtain a place within a practice. The important thing to note is that there are lots of options.

In order to become a veterinary nurse, you need to train. This can either be on a vocational route or through higher education. They both allow you to register as a veterinary nurse. The vocational course is for those who prefer practical work. This Level 3 diploma can be obtained on either a full-time or a part-time basis while you work within a veterinary practice. The degree course is longer and more academic but it will open up opportunities in research in the future and in other careers, such as teaching. The latter course should be applied for via UCAS.

The standard length of a veterinary nursing course is three years but there are some institutions that offer a four-year sandwich programme, allowing you to work while training. There are a number of RCVS-accredited veterinary nursing qualifications, including:

Anglia Ruskin University

- FdSc Veterinary Nursing with Applied Animal Behaviour (3 years)
- BSc (Hons) Veterinary Nursing with Applied Animal Behaviour (4 years)

University of Brighton

- FdSc Veterinary Nursing (3 years)

University of Bristol

- BSc (Hons) Veterinary Nursing and Bioveterinary Science (4 years)
- BSc (Hons) Veterinary Nursing and Companion Animal Behaviour (4 years)

University of Central Lancashire

- FdSc Veterinary Nursing (3 years)

Coventry University

- BSc (Hons) Veterinary Nursing (4 years)
- FdSc Veterinary Nursing (3 years)

University of Chester

- BSc (Hons) Veterinary Nursing (3 years)

Edinburgh Napier University

- BSc (Hons) Veterinary Nursing (4 years)

University of Glasgow

- Scottish BSc in Veterinary Nursing (SQF Level 9) (3 years)
- Scottish BSc (Hons) in Veterinary Nursing (SQF Level 9) (4 years)

Harper Adams University

- BSc (Hons) Veterinary Nursing
- BSc (Hons) Veterinary Nursing with Companion Animal Behaviour
- BSc (Hons) Veterinary Nursing with Small Animal Rehabilitation

Hartpury University

- BSc (Hons) Veterinary Nursing with integrated placement year (4 years)
- BSc (Hons) Equine Veterinary Nursing with integrated placement year (4 years)
- BSc Veterinary Nursing with integrated placement year (4 years)
- BSc Equine Veterinary Nursing with integrated placement year (3 years)
- Diploma in Professional Studies in Veterinary Nursing
- Diploma in Professional Studies in Equine Veterinary Nursing

Middlesex University

- BSc (Hons) Veterinary Nursing (3 years)
- BSc (Hons) Veterinary Nursing with Foundation Year (4 years)

Nottingham Trent University

- FdSc Veterinary Nursing (3 years)

Oxford Brookes University

- FdSc Veterinary Nursing (3 years)

University of Plymouth

- FdSc Veterinary Nursing (3 years)

University of Portsmouth

- FdSc Veterinary Nursing Science (3 years)

Royal Agricultural University

- FdSc Veterinary Nursing (3 years)

The University of London

- FdSc in Veterinary Nursing (3 years)

University of South Wales

- Foundation Degree in Veterinary Nursing (3 years)

SQA, Glasgow

- HND in Veterinary Nursing (2 years)

University of Wales, Trinity St David

- BSc (Hons) Veterinary Nursing (4 years)

University of the West of England

- FdSc Veterinary Nursing Science (3 years)
- FdSc Equine Veterinary Nursing (3 years)
- BSc (Hons) Veterinary Nursing Science (4 years)
- Diploma in Professional Studies Veterinary Nursing Small Animal or Equine Pathway (2 years)

Wrexham Glyndwr University

- FdSc Veterinary Nursing (3 years)

Note: Courses at the University of Chester, University of Glasgow, Oxford Brookes University, Royal Agricultural University (Plumpton College Campus) and Wrexham Glyndwr University are currently provisionally accredited. They are new qualifications that have made progress towards meeting the standards of accreditation; full accreditation will be granted once the first cohort of students have completed the course.

Women in the profession

Over three times as many women are now admitted to veterinary science courses as men. Table 7 (see page 174) shows figures from UCAS' 2018 end of year cycle applicant statistics. The figures might be rough approximations this year, but in most years the split is considered to be 80% female applicants to 20% male applicants. Therefore, gents, there is a balance to be addressed here!

Women comprise about a third of all the vets in the country, but only one in five of the sole principals in general practice are women. Two explanations have been suggested for this. One is that the statistic reflects past intakes into the profession and this is changing. Another is that, whereas women are in the majority at age 26–35, they comprise only one in five of those aged 50 or over. This suggests that they leave the profession early – perhaps in order to have a family – and do not always return. The figures also hint that women are slightly more inclined than their male colleagues to work in the public sector.

Table 7 UCAS 2020 End of Cycle applicant statistics for Pre-clinical Veterinary Medicine: male and female applicants

	Applications	Accepted applicants
Men	1,900	275
Women	7,865	1,175
Total	**9,765**	**1,450**

Source: www.ucas.com.

The Society of Practising Veterinary Surgeons has reported that the gender pay gap has decreased in recent years, but it has most recently reported that there is a gender pay gap of 19%, with male vets' annual salaries averaging at £50,750 and female vets' salaries averaging at £40,960. When considering hourly paid rates, male veterinarians are consistently paid more, typically 18.65% higher. Similarly, at the most senior level, male veterinarians get paid 20% more on average than female veterinarians in equal positions. These figures highlight the inequality for women working in the profession, which is indicative of the wider issue across all UK employment sectors currently.

UCAS Tariff

The UCAS Tariff is used by about one third of universities in their offer conditions to students, instead of asking for specific grades. Not all universities use the Tariff and it is highly unlikely that it will be used for veterinary medicine; however, for some veterinary nursing courses, entry requirements are quoted in Tariff points. Universities are more likely to stipulate grades rather than points, mostly because the points do not necessarily equate to the grades. There is the possibility though that they might ask for grades as well as points if they are using the new Tariff, i.e. a minimum requirement in a certain subject. The Tariff system for the main post-16 qualifications can be calculated using Table 8 (opposite).

Table 8 UCAS Tariff

A level	AS	IB HL	IB SL	EPQ	Pre U	Scottish Advanced Higher	Scottish Higher	Irish Leaving Certificate
A* = 56	–	7 = 56	7 = 28	A* = 28	D1 = 56	A = 56	A = 33	H1 = 36
A = 48	A = 20	6 = 48	6 = 24	A = 24	D2 = 56	B = 48	B = 27	H2 = 30
B = 40	B = 16	5 = 32	5 = 16	B = 20	D3 = 52	C = 40	C = 21	H3 = 24
C = 32	C = 12	4 = 24	4 = 12	C = 16	M1 = 44	D = 32	D = 15	H4 = 18
D = 24	D = 10	3 = 12	3 = 6	D = 12	M2 = 40	–	–	H5 = 12
E = 16	E = 6	–	–	E = 8	M3 = 36	–	–	H6 = 9
–	–	–	–	–	P1 = 28	–	–	–
–	–	–	–	–	P2 = 24	–	–	–
–	–	–	–	–	P3 = 20	–	–	–

Source: www.ucas.com
We acknowledge UCAS' contribution of this information. For further details of all qualifications awarded UCAS Tariff points see the UCAS website. Note that the Tariff is constantly updated and new qualifications are added every year.

Summing up

Many students are interested in becoming veterinary surgeons. For some it will remain a pipe dream either because they lack the ability or skill, or because their ideas about being a veterinary surgeon are not rooted in reality. However, there are real opportunities for those who are motivated and determined to reach their goal. The competition is intense but not impossible, and prospective students should be encouraged to explore the veterinary option early by seeking practical experience. As one vet put it: 'See a farm, get your wellies dirty, experience some blood and gore, and see that the life of a vet is not all about cuddly puppies!' This will test both resolve and suitability.

The demand for veterinary services and research-related activities is strong and is increasing. Market forces do dictate the number of places in veterinary schools, but funding limitations imposed by the higher education funding councils are also a controlling factor. Nevertheless, the profession of veterinary surgeon retains its popularity among young people. It is not because of the money, the car, or accommodation – which is often next to the practice, ready for instant call-outs. Nor can the hours be the attraction: the provision of a 24-hour service to the public is mandatory. Rather, it is probably the sense that being a vet is a way of life rather than a job.

As we have been discussing, however, Brexit is expected to have a significant impact on the veterinary profession, in terms of education, regulation and workforce planning. It is likely to also have an effect on research, surveillance, animal movements and animal welfare. However, only time will tell the impact and much will be clearer as the details are ironed out in 2021.

The unique skills a vet requires

A vet is many things – skilled surgeon, business manager, counsellor and confidant. Vets know that their animals are often the most important thing in their clients' lives. They have tremendous responsibility for the animals, whether in sickness or in health, and when all other options have failed they have the authority and power vested in them by law to take the animal's life. They devote their lives to animal welfare but their role is not based on sentimentality. Find out whether it is the life for you, and, if it is, go for it.

> **Fact:** Horses can't vomit.

12| Don't count your chickens before they've hatched

Further information

Don't make the mistake of believing that you know enough, because you can always find out more. If you want to be the cat that got the cream, do your research. You will be more likely to get in to your first choice of university if you do your own investigations about where you want to go. Remember, there is no harm in entering into a dialogue with an admissions tutor if you are asking pertinent and considered questions. An elephant never forgets and neither does an admissions tutor.

Listed below are the contact details of the veterinary schools in the UK and websites of other organisations that might help your research.

Veterinary schools in the UK

Aberystwyth
School of Veterinary Science
Penglais Campus
Penglais
Aberystwyth
Ceredigion SY23 3FL
Tel: 01970 623111
Email: vet-info@aber.ac.uk
Website: www.aber.ac.uk/en/vet-sci

Bristol
Bristol Veterinary School
Langford House
Langford
Bristol BS40 5DU
Tel (veterinary admissions): 0117 394 1649
Email: choosebristol-ug@bristol.ac.uk (undergraduate); vet-student-admin@bristol.ac.uk (veterinary science course queries); admin@bristol.ac.uk (veterinary nursing course queries)
Website: www.bristol.ac.uk/vetscience

Cambridge
Veterinary Admission Enquiries Adviser
Department of Veterinary Medicine
University of Cambridge
Madingley Road
Cambridge CB3 0ES
Tel: 01223 337701
Email: admissions.enquiries@vet.cam.ac.uk
Website: www.vet.cam.ac.uk

Edinburgh
The Admissions Officer
Royal (Dick) School of Veterinary Studies
University of Edinburgh
Easter Bush Campus
Midlothian EH25 9RG
Tel: 0131 651 7305
Email: vetug@ed.ac.uk
Website: www.ed.ac.uk/vet

Glasgow
Admissions Office
School of Veterinary Medicine
College of Medical, Veterinary and Life Sciences
University of Glasgow
Garscube Campus
Bearsden Road
Glasgow G61 1QH
Tel: 0141 330 5706
Email: reception@vet.gla.ac.uk
Website: www.gla.ac.uk/schools/vet

Harper & Keele
Harper Adams University
Harper Adams Veterinary School
Newport
Shropshire
TF10 8NB
Tel: 01952 820280

Keele University
Keele Veterinary School
Staffordshire
ST5 5BG
Tel: 01782 732000

Email: admissions@hkvets.ac.uk or office@hkvets.ac.uk
Website: www.harperkeelevetschool.ac.uk

Liverpool
Admissions Sub-Dean
School of Veterinary Science
Thompson Yates Building
University of Liverpool
Liverpool L69 3GB
Tel: 0151 794 4797
Email: vetadmit@liverpool.ac.uk
Website: www.liv.ac.uk/veterinary-science

London
The Registry
Royal Veterinary College
University of London
Royal College Street
London NW1 0TU
Tel: 020 7468 5147
Email: admissions@rvc.ac.uk
Website: www.rvc.ac.uk

Nottingham
Admissions Team
School of Veterinary Medicine and Science
University of Nottingham
Sutton Bonington Campus
College Road
Sutton Bonington LE12 5RD
Tel: 0115 951 6116
Email: veterinary-enquiries@nottingham.ac.uk
Website: www.nottingham.ac.uk/vet

Surrey
School of Veterinary Medicine
Faculty of Health and Medical Sciences
Vet School Main Building (VSM)
University of Surrey
Daphne Jackson Road
Guildford
Surrey GU2 7AL
Tel: 01483 683882
Email: vetschool@surrey.ac.uk
Website: www.surrey.ac.uk/school-veterinary-medicine

Other contacts and sources of information

Useful organisations and websites

- **Animal Welfare Foundation:** www.bva-awf.org.uk
- **Blue Cross:** www.bluecross.org.uk
- **British Equine Veterinary Association:** www.beva.org.uk
- **British Veterinary Association** (this is the national representative body for the British veterinary profession): www.bva.co.uk
- **Department for Environment, Food and Rural Affairs (Defra):** www.defra.gov.uk
- **People's Dispensary for Sick Animals:** www.pdsa.org.uk

Royal College of Veterinary Surgeons
Belgravia House
62–64 Horseferry Road
London SW1P 2AF
Tel: 020 7222 2001
Email: info@rcvs.org.uk
Website: www.rcvs.org.uk

St George's University
University Centre
Grenada
West Indies
Tel: 0800 169 9061 ext. 1413
Email: sguenrolment@sgu.edu
Website: www.sgu.edu

University of Medicine in Kosice, Slovak Republic
Recruitment (XLNC)
Application to Faculty of Medicine
UPJS in Kosice
Matuskova 18
Trieda SNP 1
04011 Kosice
Slovak Republic
Tel: +42 155 234 3319
Email: info@medicinekosice.eu
Website: www.upjs.sk/en/facility-of-medicine

Society of Practising Veterinary Surgeons
www.spvs.org.uk
Provides advice to veterinary surgeons.

Universities and Colleges Admissions Service
www.ucas.com

Vet Times
www.vettimes.co.uk
Online database and resource.

GOV.UK
www.gov.uk/student-finance
Information on student loans and grants.

The Department of Agriculture and Rural Development (Northern Ireland)
www.dardni.gov.uk

The Student Room
www.thestudentroom.co.uk

Member of the Royal College of Veterinary Surgeons
www.mrcvs.co.uk

WikiVet
https://en.wikivet.net/Veterinary_Education_Online

World Organisation for Animal Health
www.oie.int/animal-health-in-the-world/oie-listed-diseases-2016

Courses

VetCam
www.vet.cam.ac.uk/study/vet/vetcam Tel: 01223 330811
Two-day residential 'Introduction to Veterinary Science in Cambridge' course, held in March.

Vetsim
www.workshop-uk.net/vetsim
Conference organised by Workshop Conferences for interested sixth-formers and held annually in Nottingham.

FutureLearn
www.futurelearn.com/courses/vet-school-application-support
Virtual work experience and exploring the veterinary profession. An online course accepted by universities in place of work experience in the context of Covid-19.

Publications

Getting into Oxford & Cambridge: 2022 Entry, Matthew Carmody, Trotman Education.
Packed with essential advice to help you win one of the fiercely sought-after places at Oxbridge, this guide tells you everything you need to know to make a successful application. Featuring case studies from current students throughout, it also gives an insight into what studying at Oxford and Cambridge is really like.

HEAP 2022: University Degree Course Offers, 51st edition, Brian Heap, Trotman Education.
Lists the target offers and admissions details for over 100 main degree subjects at universities and colleges across the UK, helping applicants to choose the right course and win their place.

How to Complete Your UCAS Application: 2022 Entry, 33rd edition, Ray Le Tarouilly, Trotman Education.
Works through the application procedure step by step using examples, and includes information on how to avoid the most common mistakes and how to write a winning personal statement.

Glossary

Admissions tutor
The person in charge of your application.

American Veterinary Medical Association (AVMA)
The AVMA represents US veterinarians, providing information, publications and resources such as training courses.

Animal Health and Veterinary Laboratories Agency (AHVLA)
Working on behalf of Defra throughout Great Britain, the AHVLA was established to ensure animal health and welfare and public health.

Animal husbandry
An agricultural term meaning breeding and raising livestock.

Bachelor of Veterinary Medicine (BVetMed)
A bachelor's degree for studies in the United Kingdom. Most courses are five years in length, although Cambridge has a six-year course and chooses to award a Bachelor of Arts (BA) after three years, followed by a Bachelor of Veterinary Medicine (VetMB) after six years.

Bovine spongiform encephalopathy (BSE)
Commonly referred to as mad cow disease, BSE is a neurological disease that affects the brains of cattle. The human form of the disease is Creutzfeldt–Jakob disease (CJD).

Bovine tuberculosis (bTB)
Bovine tuberculosis is a serious disease in cattle. It is said to be commonly spread by badgers, which are a protected species, and therefore the debate remains over whether badgers should be culled.

British Equine Veterinary Association (BEVA)
The BEVA is the leading body for the equine veterinary profession. It ensures high standards throughout the profession, has 2,400 members globally and also runs outstanding continuing professional development (CPD) courses.

Clinical years
The third and fourth years of veterinary medicine degree courses.

Continuing professional development (CPD)
The Royal College of Veterinary Surgeons' Code of Professional Conduct for Veterinary Surgeons states that veterinary surgeons have

a responsibility to 'maintain and develop the knowledge and skills relevant to their professional practice and competence'. A minimum amount of 105 hours over an ongoing three-year period is recommended for CPD, with an average of 35 hours per year.

Department for Environment, Food and Rural Affairs (Defra)
The government department that looks after environmental protection, agriculture, food production standards, fisheries and rural communities in the United Kingdom. It is responsible for maintaining high standards within the industries.

Department of Agriculture and Rural Development (DARDNI)
For information on veterinary medicine in Northern Ireland.

European Association of Establishments for Veterinary Education (EAEVE)
The EAEVE aims to harmonise the standards of veterinary tuition in the European Union, giving confidence to members of the public and veterinary professionals.

Extramural rotations (EMR)
EMR are undertaken by students studying at veterinary school; the time is divided between farming work and experience in veterinary practice.

Extramural studies (EMS)
EMS are studies that take place outside the university setting. The Royal College of Veterinary Surgeons states that students must complete 38 weeks of EMS during their course: 12 weeks of pre-clinical and 26 weeks of clinical placements.

Foot-and-mouth disease (FMD)
FMD is a viral disease that affects cattle, pigs, sheep, goats and deer. Hedgehogs and rats can also become infected, and people, cats, dogs and game animals can carry infected material. FMD is more contagious than any other animal disease, and the mortality rate among young animals is high.

Fresher
A first-year undergraduate student.

FVE
Federation of Veterinarians of Europe.

Integrated course
A course that teaches lots of different disciplines which all come together in the final year of study. The individual elements are taught by specialists in disciplines ranging from pharmacology to anatomy.

International English Language Testing System (IELTS)
An English test used to determine the level of language ability for international students. A typical score of 7.0 is required.

Intramural rotations (IMR)
IMR take place in the clinical years of veterinary medicine, and are designed to develop and utilise skills you have previously learnt. You will work in clinical teams and have access to clinical records. This will encourage you to present a professional image.

Master of Science (MSc)
The MSc is typically a taught programme over one or two years, depending on the university.

Methicillin-resistant *Staphylococcus aureus* (MRSA)
MRSA, commonly known as the 'superbug', is a human-based infection found in hospitals but it can also colonise and cause infections in pets and farm animals.

Multiple choice questions (MCQs)
MCQs are used in some veterinary examinations.

Natural Sciences Admissions Assessment (NSAA)
This examination is taken by students who have applied for veterinary medicine at the University of Cambridge.

North American Veterinary Licensing Examination (NAVLE)
In order to practise in North America, students must pass the NAVLE.

People's Dispensary for Sick Animals (PDSA)
The PDSA is a veterinary charity that offers healthcare for a range of animals.

Pharmacodynamics
The study of the mechanism of the action of drugs and how they affect the body.

Pharmacokinetics
The study of the absorption, distribution, metabolism and excretion of drugs.

Pre-clinical years
The first two years of veterinary medicine.

Professional Development Phase (PDP)
The first year after completing your degree is the PDP, when you are expected to develop your skills.

Royal College of Veterinary Surgeons (RCVS)
The regulatory body for all veterinary professionals in the United Kingdom. The RCVS's role is to ensure the health and welfare of animals and the efficient practice of veterinary professionals and to provide an impartial opinion on animal health and disease as well as on the latest debates.

Royal Society for the Prevention of Cruelty to Animals (RSPCA)

The leading UK charity specialising in the care, control and rescue of animals.

Royal Veterinary College (RVC)

The oldest and largest of the veterinary schools in the United Kingdom and one of the world's leading specialist veterinary schools.

Therapeutics

The use of drugs in the prevention and treatment of disease.

Universities and Colleges Admissions Service (UCAS)

The central body through which students apply to veterinary schools; you do not apply to the universities directly. You can choose four veterinary courses and one non-veterinary course.

Veterinary Laboratories Agency (VLA)

Centre set up to operate and support control schemes in the interests of public health, to monitor developments and give early warning of any disease problems or dangers to the safety of the food chain; now part of the Animal Health and Veterinary Laboratories Agency.

Veterinary Medicines Directorate (VMD)

The VMD deals with the licensing of drugs.

> **Fact:** 'The quick brown fox jumps over a lazy dog' – it does this while using every letter of the alphabet.